The Flat Tax

HOOVER CLASSICS

The Hoover Classics series will reissue selected books of lasting merit and influence from the list of previous Hoover Institution Press publications. The aim of the series is to engender new interest in these titles and expand the readership to a wider audience—in some cases, to a new generation. Additionally, it is hoped that by extending the life of these books, they will continue to contribute to free discussion and debate on important issues of public policy and historical understanding.

The Flat Tax, by Robert E. Hall and Alvin Rabushka, is the inaugural selection in this series.

Contents

The Flat Tax's
Silver Anniversary

FIRST PROPOSED 25 years ago, the flat tax has proven most influential in the unlikeliest of places: state capitals—and the capitals of other nations.

On December 10, 1981, Robert Hall and I first published on the editorial page of the *Wall Street Journal* our proposal to replace the federal income tax with a low, simple, flat tax. The article, titled "A Proposal to Simplify Our Tax System," displayed the iconic postcard that became the symbol of the flat tax. Our system was so simple that an individual or business could file a federal income tax return on a postcard-sized form.

The flat tax picked up considerable steam in the United States during the next few years, culminating in President Reagan's Tax Reform Act of 1986. Two rates of 15 and 28 percent replaced multiple tax brackets with a top rate of 50 percent. From that point, the flat tax lost momentum. In 1990, in exchange for spending cuts that failed to materialize, President George H.W. Bush signed the Omnibus Budget Reconciliation Act that included a 31 percent rate on "the rich." On August 10, 1993, President Clinton signed a similar act, which passed the Congress by exactly one vote in the House of Representatives, adding two further brackets of 36 and 39.6 percent.

When control of Congress passed into Republican hands in 1995, House majority leader Dick Armey put the flat tax back into the limelight. Armey, Steve Forbes, and other political leaders talked up the flat tax during the next few years, but it never came to the floor of the House or Senate for a vote.

Ideas, however, have a way of cropping up again in unexpected places. Against the advice of Western economists, the newly independent country of Estonia enacted a flat tax effective January 1, 1994. It set the rate at 26 percent to balance its budget. It has since lowered the rate on several occasions, and the tax is scheduled to fall to 20 percent in 2009. Estonia has also abolished its corporate income tax, only imposing the same flat rate on distributed dividends. Estonia's budget has been in surplus since 2001.

Estonia set off an avalanche of flat taxes: in 1995 by Latvia (25 percent) and Lithuania (33 percent, to be reduced to 24 percent before the end of the decade). But the big story was Russia, which adopted a 13 percent flat tax, down from a top rate of 30 percent, effective January 1, 2001. In the four-plus years since it was adopted, real ruble revenues, adjusted for inflation, have more than doubled.

Next came Serbia in 2003, with a comprehensive 14 percent flat tax on personal and corporate income. Taking a page from Russia's playbook, in 2004 Ukraine replaced its five-bracket income tax, ranging from 10–40 percent, with a 13 percent flat tax. That year Slovakia also replaced its five-bracket tax, ranging from 10–38 percent, with a 19 percent flat tax on both personal and corporate income. Double taxation of corporate income was eliminated.

Georgia followed Slovakia with a 12 percent flat tax and Romania with a 16 percent flat tax on both personal and corporate income, both taking hold January 1, 2005. Romania's Finance Ministry reported that income-tax revenue for the first eight months of 2006 greatly exceeded estimates and that the state budget had a significant surplus at the end of July, amounting to 1.12 percent of the gross domestic product.

The flat tax continued to pick up steam in 2006, spreading beyond Central and Eastern Europe. On February 1, 2006, President Kurmanbek Bakiyev of Kyrgyzstan signed into law modifications in the country's tax code that established a 10 percent flat tax. It replaced the current corporate tax of 20 percent and the individual income tax with rates between 10 and 20 percent. Shortly thereafter, the president of neighboring Kazakhstan said his country would consider a flat tax in 2007.

Last July, the people of Macedonia voted to establish their own country. One of the main pillars of new Prime Minister Nikola Gruevski's 100-point reform program was a flat tax, which came into being in January 2007 at 12 percent—and is scheduled to diminish to 10 percent in 2008. It replaced a corporate tax rate of 15 percent and personal income tax rates that ranged between 15 and 24 percent. The purpose of the low 10 percent flat tax is to give Macedonia one of the lowest tax rates in Europe to help it emulate the success of Estonia, Latvia, and Lithuania, which experienced strong economic growth after the adoption of their flat taxes.

Also in July, the tiny island of Mauritius, located in

the Indian Ocean about 1,500 miles off the southeast coast of Africa, approved its 2006–2007 budget. The signal feature of it is the advent, on July 1, 2009, of a 15 percent flat tax on personal and corporate income. That tax will replace the current personal income tax of two rates, 15 percent on taxable income to 25,000 rupees (about $800) and 25 percent on the rest. It will eliminate much of the complexity and many of the current deductions and credits in the current system. The 15 percent flat tax will also replace the existing 25 percent tax on corporate income.

In late May 2006, Kuwait indicated that it was studying a proposal to introduce an income tax at a flat rate of 10 percent. The draft law is to be studied by the cabinet and, if approved, sent to the country's Parliament for consideration.

In 2006, Mongolia's parliament enacted a far-reaching tax reform. Effective January 1, 2007, personal income is taxed at a 10 percent flat rate, with a tax-free allowance of MNT (Mongolia Tugriks) 84,000 ($866/year). Previously, from May 1, 1997, personal income was taxed at three rates of 10, 20, and 40 percent, with the top rate reduced to 30 percent in 2004, and an allowance of 48,000 MNT ($495/year). The decision to adopt a 10 percent flat tax reflected several important principles of tax policy: decreasing the tax burden on individuals, reducing the underground economy, broadening the tax base, increasing the efficiency of tax collection, and improving compliance by clarifying and simplifying the tax laws.

Several other developments warrant mention.

Guernsey, a British Crown dependency in the Channel Islands off the west coast of France, has had for many years a 20 percent flat tax on corporate and personal income. Last July, its Parliament approved a zero corporate tax rate and capped the maximum tax on individuals at £250,000. The cap means that tax rates decline once taxable income exceeds £1,250,000, transforming the territory's flat tax into a degressive tax.

The new president of Mexico, Felipe Calderón, has pledged to introduce a flat tax to simplify Mexico's tax code and improve tax collection, which at just 11 percent of gross domestic product is insufficient to fund social development and improve the country's physical infrastructure.

In the United States, the federal income tax has been further complicated by something known as the alternative minimum tax (AMT). The AMT was originally enacted to prevent individuals from eliminating most of their federal income-tax liabilities through numerous deductions and tax shelters. Under the AMT, taxpayers pay the higher of either the AMT, assessed at a flat rate of 28 percent, or the regular income tax.

Something quite new and different has been happening at the state level. Before 2006, six states maintained flat-rate income taxes: Colorado (4.63 percent), Illinois (3.0 percent), Indiana (3.4 percent), Massachusetts (5.3 percent), Michigan (3.07 percent), and Pennsylvania (3.07 percent). Last year, Rhode Island and Utah adopted optional flat taxes of 5.5 and 5.35 percent, respectively. In contrast with the federal AMT, in which taxpayers must pay the higher of the AMT or regular income tax, state taxpayers in Rhode Island and Utah can choose to pay the lower of the flat tax without any deductions or the standard income tax with deductions. Other state legislatures are exploring similar optional flat taxes.

Perhaps the movement to optional flat taxes in the states will breathe new life into support for a federal flat tax, but one with a rate of 19 percent that Robert Hall and I first proposed—or even lower. Certainly not the AMT's 28 percent!

Alvin Rabushka
The David and Joan Traitel Senior Fellow
at the Hoover Institution
2007

Preface

SINCE 1981, when we first introduced our flat-tax plan, we have talked about it on more than a thousand occasions. These include hearings before the Joint Economic Committee, the Senate Finance Committee, and the House Ways and Means Committee; discussions with dozens of members of Congress; briefings at the Department of the Treasury and with the White House staff; seminars and lectures at dozens of universities and colleges; interviews with hundreds of newspaper and magazine reporters and television crews in the United States and overseas; dozens of appearances on call-in radio shows around the country; and countless speeches before a variety of professional and civic organizations. We have heard tirades of criticism of the current federal income tax and received much praise for our flat-tax alternative. We have also heard every possible objection to our flat-tax plan and have tried to answer each of them. We remain convinced, as ever, that the adoption of the flat tax would give an enormous boost to the U.S. economy by dramatically improving incentives to work, save, invest, and take entrepreneurial risks. The flat tax would save taxpayers hundreds of billions in direct and indirect compliance costs. It would also shift billions of dollars from investments that reduce taxes to those that produce goods and services.

This book sets forth the flat-tax plan we have developed. It is, we believe, the most fair, efficient, simple, and workable plan on the table.

Under our flat tax, all income would be taxed once and only once, at a uniform low rate of 19 percent. Our plan is fair to ordinary Americans because it would permit a tax-free allowance of $25,500 for a family of four. The family would pay a tax of 19 percent on its earnings above that allowance. Millions of U.S. residents would no longer pay any income taxes. All wage earners would pay less tax under our flat tax than under the current system.

Our flat tax would eliminate the distortions of the present tax treatment of business. It would replace a hodgepodge of depreciation schedules with an effective investment incentive, a first-year write-off. It would reduce the current corporate tax of 35 percent to 19 percent. It would eliminate double taxation of business income by ending taxation of dividends and capital gains.

Our flat tax adheres to the principle of a consumption tax: people are taxed on what they take out of the economy, not on what they put in.

Our flat tax is not an academic abstraction. We have designed tax forms, rewritten the Internal Revenue Code, and worked out all the practical details. The flat tax has withstood the scrutiny of leading experts on taxation and has been endorsed enthusiastically by many of them. Both the *New York Times* and the *Wall Street Journal* have endorsed our flat tax. Both Republicans and Democrats have introduced it as bills in previous sessions of Congress.

Opponents of the flat tax have charged that it would

imperil homeowners and the real estate industry, reduce charitable contributions, and provide a windfall to the rich. These are charges we take seriously. We will show that they are mistaken. Adopting the flat tax would improve the overall performance of the economy. Housing and charitable giving would flourish. Everyone's after-tax income would rise.

All designers of rival tax plans agree that the tax base must be broadened and that tax rates must be lowered. Our flat tax meets the tests of efficiency, equity, and simplicity better than every other plan that has been proposed.

In the previous edition of our book, we thanked those individuals and organizations that helped us formulate our ideas, promote the flat tax, and bring it before Congress and other public officials. To those previous acknowledgments, we add the following: Bruce Herschensohn, who made our flat-tax proposal a centerpiece of his 1992 California campaign for the U.S. Senate; Congressman Dick Armey (and his legislative assistant, Andrew A. Laperriere), who introduced a variation of our flat tax in the 103rd Congress; and Malcom S. Forbes Jr., who has remained a staunch supporter of our flat tax for many years. Bruce Bartlett graciously supplied us with an extensive bibliography; Christopher Wilkins and Christopher Sleet provided invaluable research assistance.

The Hoover Institution has supported every phase

xvi   The Flat Tax

of our work, and we are grateful to be able to work in its world-class facilities. We want to thank Director John Raisian for his many kind words each time he has introduced either or both of us at numerous institution events.

1. Meet the Federal Income Tax

The tax code has become near incomprehensible except to specialists.
> Daniel Patrick Moynihan, Chairman,
> Senate Finance Committee, August 11, 1994

I would repeal the entire Internal Revenue Code and start over.
> Shirley Peterson, Former Commissioner,
> Internal Revenue Service, August 3, 1994

Tax laws are so complex that mechanical rules have caused some lawyers to lose sight of the fact that their stock-in-trade as lawyers should be sound judgment, not an ability to recall an obscure paragraph and manipulate its language to derive unintended tax benefits.
> Margaret Milner Richardson, Commissioner,
> Internal Revenue Service, August 10, 1994

It will be of little avail to the people, that the laws are made by men of their own choice, if the laws be so voluminous that they cannot be read, or so incoherent that they cannot be understood; if they be repealed or revised before they are promulgated, or undergo such incessant changes that no man, who knows what the law is to-day, can guess what it will be to-morrow.
> Alexander Hamilton or James Madison,
> *The Federalist*, no. 62

THE FEDERAL INCOME TAX is a complete mess. It's not efficient. It's not fair. It's not simple. It's not comprehensible. It fosters tax avoidance and cheating. It costs billions of dollars to administer. It costs taxpayers billions of dollars in time spent filling out tax forms and other forms of compliance. It costs the economy billions of dollars in lost output of goods and services from investments being made for tax rather than for economic purposes. It involves tens of thousands of lawyers and lobbyists getting tax benefits for their clients instead of performing productive work. It can't find ten serious economists to defend it. It is not worth saving.

How large are the costs of the federal income tax? They are larger than the federal budget deficit, larger than the Defense Department, larger than Social Security, perhaps as large as the combined budgets of the fifty states.

The tax system was better in 1986. Not perfect, but better. That year, President Ronald Reagan signed the landmark Tax Reform Act of 1986. It reduced the top marginal rate of taxation on personal income to 28 percent—down from an appalling 70 percent in 1980. It did away with more than $100 billion in wasteful tax shelters. It dramatically improved incentives to work, save, and invest. But it barely lasted four years.

What happened? Two presidents undid the 1986 act. First was George Bush. He stood side by side with the bipartisan congressional leadership as he signed the Omnibus Budget Reconciliation Act of 1990. He proclaimed $500 billion in deficit reduction over five years, half in higher taxes, including a 31 percent tax rate on "the rich." Second was Bill Clinton. In his 1992 campaign for the White House, he promised a middle-class tax cut. Once in office, he, too, became captivated with "deficit reduction." On August 10, 1993, he signed the Omnibus Budget Reconciliation Act of 1993, which passed the U.S. Congress by exactly one vote in the House of Representatives. It promised another $500 billion in deficit reduction, half in higher taxes, and included two higher tax rates on "the rich" to ensure that "those who benefited unfairly in the 1980s from the Reagan tax-rate reductions paid their 'fair share' in the 1990s." In 1986, the income tax had just two rates: 15 and 28 percent. By 1995, it had five rates: 15.0, 28.0, 31.0, 36.0, and 39.6 percent.

The Declaration of Independence was in large measure a bill of particulars against British taxation. Its roots are found in the first Stamp Act Congress of 1766, when colonial leaders met to protest the British Stamp Tax. Other unpopular British taxes included a host of customs duties on paper, dyes, glass, and tea and a disguised tax on owners of property.

It's time for another Declaration of Independence, this time from an unfair, costly, complicated federal income tax. The alternative, as we argue in this book, is a low, simple flat tax.

WHAT'S AHEAD

The object of this book is to persuade you that a low, simple flat tax is the best possible replacement for the current federal income tax. Here's how we intend to proceed.

This chapter indicts the current federal income tax. In it we document the follow charges:

- The federal income tax is too complicated for ordinary taxpayers to understand.

- The federal income tax costs taxpayers more than a hundred billion dollars in compliance.

- The federal income tax costs the economy tens of billions of dollars in wasteful investments.

- The federal income tax is responsible for more than a hundred billion dollars in tax cheating.

- The federal income tax encourages lawyers and lobbyists to seek tax favors from Congress instead of earning an honest living.

Chapter 1 concludes with a brief history of the federal income tax.

Chapter 2 is all about "fairness." We have learned, during the past fifteen years, that the most dangerous critique of the flat tax is the emotionally laden charge that it's not fair. We intend to dispose of this false, mistaken charge once and for all. Indeed, we claim that the flat tax is the fairest tax of all. To show that the flat tax is indeed fair requires a thorough discussion of tax terminology. We define such crucial terms as *tax base, marginal tax rates, tax burden, consumption taxes,* and *equity,* among others. In chapter 2 we also show that the flat tax is the only proposed replacement for the current income tax that has received support from opposite ends of the spectrum: in politics, from Jerry Brown and Dick Armey; in the media, from the *New York Times* and the *Wall Street Journal.* Thus, on the issue of a well-designed tax system, our flat tax commands a broader array of support than any other proposal.

Chapter 3 spells out the mechanics and logic of the flat tax. We would replace hundreds of forms and thousands of regulations with two postcard-sized tax forms, one for business firms and the other for wage and salary earners. Our flat tax solves many tax problems that have challenged academics and politicians for years: it eliminates double taxation; it improves capital formation; it correctly defines the tax base; it provides true simplification; it dramatically improves incentives; it removes millions of low-income households from the tax net; it lowers the costs of compliance; it puts a serious dent in tax cheating; it even reduces the adversarial stance of the Internal Revenue Service toward taxpayers. Chapter 3 also deals with the transition, how we get from the current federal income tax to the flat tax, including such issues as the loss of deductions for home mortgage interest and charitable contributions and the replacement of complicated depreciation schedules with straightforward expensing, 100 percent immediate write-off, of all investment.

Chapter 4 addresses the big economic issues. Adopting the flat tax will, first and foremost, increase economic growth; in other words, the economy will increase its output of goods and services. It will increase investment by promoting capital formation. It will create new jobs and increase real wages by improving incentives to work. It will reduce interest rates immediately. It will reduce future budget deficits. It will make Americans more respectful of their government. It will even reduce crime because taxpayers will become more honest in filing their annual tax returns—a useful side effect of an intelligent approach to taxation.

Chapter 5 is a handy collection of questions and answers about the flat tax. During the past fifteen years we have presented our plan to more than a thousand audiences. We have heard, we believe, almost every single conceivable objection or concern that can possibly be raised about the flat tax. Here we assemble brief answers to the most frequently asked questions.

For specialists, we include an appendix with the language of our flat-tax law and a section on notes and references.

A NIGHTMARE OF COMPLEXITY

President Jimmy Carter called the income tax "a disgrace to the human race." He was right. The best way we know to document Carter's charge is to take you on a tour of the Law School Library at Stanford University. It's a bit unnerving, as it reveals the nightmarish complexity of the income tax.

The Internal Revenue Code consumes enormous quantities of ink and paper. West Publishing Company, one of the official publishers of the federal tax code, published the 1994 code in two volumes. Volume 1 contains sections 1 to 1,000 (1,168 printed pages), and volume 2, sections 1,001 to 1,564 (210 pages). The table of contents displays 205 separate headings. West also prints a five-volume series entitled *Federal Tax Regulations 1994*, an essential companion to the tax code. Volumes 1—4, some 6,439 pages of fine print, apply to the income tax.

The *Code* and *Regulations* defy ready comprehension. A massive industry has grown up to service tax scholars, tax lawyers, tax planners, tax filers, tax accountants, and even tax collectors.

The Internal Revenue Service (IRS), the agency charged with collecting federal income taxes, has its hands full. It has in service about 480 tax forms—the best known of which is Form 1040—and has published another 280 forms to explain to you, the taxpayer, how to fill out the 480 forms. All told, it takes thousands of pages to explain the forms. Three publishing firms help out, each issuing three volumes of forms and explanations, each taking up almost a foot of shelf space.

Pausing in our tour, for the moment, we should note that the IRS sends about eight billion pages of forms and instructions a year to more than one hundred million taxpayers. Placed end to end, these pages would stretch 694,000 miles, or about twenty-eight times around the earth. The IRS despoils the environment, chopping down about 293,760 trees to print all of this paper. A postcard-sized tax form would go a long way toward saving America's forests.

The tour, in all, covers some 336 feet of shelf space. In addition to the laws and regulations, there are volume upon volume of tax court cases, journals for professors and practitioners, and books commenting on every conceivable aspect of federal income taxation. One benefit of our book is that it gives you a reasonably complete

list of sources on federal income taxation (see the notes
and references).

There are dozens of textbooks explaining the federal
income tax along with an ever-increasing number of annual tax preparation guides. There are such specialized
volumes as *Bender's 1994 Dictionary of 1040 Deductions*, which contains a nineteen-page double-column
index to refer to items in the text. No wonder the ordinary citizen feels overwhelmed and threatened by the
Internal Revenue Service. This is no way to run a tax
system.

By the way, the price of a share of stock in H & R
Block, the nation's leading tax preparation firm, increased by 20 percent in the first month following passage of the 1993 federal tax increase.

WHAT THE INCOME TAX COSTS
THE AMERICAN PEOPLE

It's hard to imagine that any group of experts, however
hard they tried, could design a worse tax system than
the one produced by our Congress. The main benefi-
ciaries of the income tax appear to be, first, the members
of the two tax-writing committees, the Senate Finance
Committee and the House Ways and Means Committee. Their chairmen lead their respective chambers in
campaign contributions; other members of the two committees typically collect twice as much in contributions
as their colleagues in the Senate and House. Second,
members of Congress share the benefits of the federal
income tax with more than seventy thousand highly paid

lobbyists in Washington, D.C., and several hundred thousand lawyers, accountants, sellers of tax shelters, software suppliers, and others who earn a living on the tax system.

The federal income tax imposes two huge costs on the American people: direct compliance costs (record keeping, learning about tax requirements, preparing, copying, and sending forms, commercial tax preparation fees, audits and correspondence, penalties, errors in processing, litigation, tax court cases, enforcement and collection) and indirect economic losses from disincentives—economists call these "deadweight losses," "excess burdens," or "welfare costs"—due to the reduction in output incurred by the complicated, high-rate federal income tax (reduction in labor supply, reduction in capital formation, reduction in new corporate formations, reduction in new business formation, failure to expand existing businesses, investments designed to reduce taxes rather than produce income, commonly known as tax avoidance, and tax evasion, just plain cheating).

Studies of the *burden of the tax system*, what it costs the economy to administer the federal income tax, are relatively new. Studies of *tax burdens*, who pays what share of income taxes, are well established. This explains, in part, the obsession with issues of fairness and why every proposed change in federal income taxes is judged in terms of who wins and who loses.

In recent years, a growing spate of studies of the burden of the tax system, both in direct compliance costs and in indirect economic losses to the economy, reveals a disturbing result: The total costs are much higher than anyone has ever imagined. To give but one example, about fifty years ago, the Internal Revenue Service estimated the compliance burden of individuals at 1.2 percent of federal tax revenues; in 1969, the figure was raised to 2.4 percent of income tax revenues; in 1977, the Commission on Federal Paperwork raised the estimate to 3 percent; and in 1985, an IRS-commissioned study by Arthur D. Little concluded that the 5.4 billion hours of work expended in the taxpayers' paperwork burden for filing business and individual returns amounted to a staggering 24.4 percent of income tax revenues, the incredible sum of $159 billion. (These results, and the results of other academic and professional studies, are summarized in a 1993 book by James L. Payne, *Costly Returns*.)

The science of estimating compliance costs and indirect economic losses is, as noted, relatively new, and findings differ widely. Payne, for example, estimated the total costs of the federal tax system in 1985 at $363 billion, or 65 percent of actual collections. Others have reached higher costs in some categories of compliance and lower costs in others. In this chapter, we try our hand at estimating these costs, some directly and others by citing the best evidence available.

DIRECT COSTS OF COMPLIANCE

Let's take the most familiar items, federal income tax Forms 1040, 1040A, and 1040EZ. In 1994, the IRS reported preliminary statistics on 1992 returns. Altogether, taxpayers filed 113.8 million returns; of these, 65.7 million were the full Form 1040 (about 58 percent), 28.9 million Form 1040A (25 percent), and 19.1 million Form 1040EZ (17 percent). These percentages have been stable since 1990. Now turn to page 4 of the Internal Revenue Service *1993 1040 Forms and Instructions*, "Privacy Act and Paperwork Reduction Act Notice." It includes a section titled The Time It Takes to Prepare Your Return. Here's what it says.

> We [the IRS] try to create forms and instructions that are accurate and can be easily understood. Often this is difficult to do because some of the tax laws enacted by Congress are very complex. For some people with income mostly from wages, filling in the forms is easy. For others who have businesses, pensions, stocks, rental income, or other investments, it is more difficult.

Page 4 includes a table titled Estimated Preparation Time, which is the average time required of taxpayers. We have reproduced it as table 1.1.

The table, of course, is incomplete. It omits numerous forms. The standard 1040 booklet includes, in addition to those in the table, Form 4562, Depreciation and Amortization, which includes eight pages of instructions in the 1040 booklet, and Form 8829, Expenses for Business Use of Your Home. The IRS estimates that it takes more than forty-six hours to complete Form 4562 and about two and a half hours for Form 8829. (Perhaps to avoid frightening taxpayers even more, the Form 1040 booklet does not include such commonly used forms as 2106, 2119, 2210, 2441, 3903, 4868, 5329, 8283, 8582,

Table 1.1 Estimated Preparation Time

Form	Record Keeping	Learning about the Law or the Form	Preparing the Form	Copying, Assembling, and Sending the Form to the IRS
Form 1040	3 hr., 8 min.	2 hr., 47 min.	3 hr., 44 min.	53 min.
Sch. A (1040)	2 hr., 32 min.	24 min.	1 hr., 9 min.	27 min.
Sch. B (1040)	33 min.	8 min.	17 min.	20 min.
Sch. C (1040)	6 hr., 26 min.	1 hr., 10 min.	2 hr., 5 min.	35 min.
Sch. C-EZ (1040)	46 min.	4 min.	18 min.	20 min.
Sch. D (1040)	51 min.	49 min.	1 hr., 19 min.	48 min.
Sch. E (1040)	2 hr., 52 min.	1 hr., 6 min.	1 hr., 16 min.	35 min.
Sch. EIC (1040)	40 min.	19 min.	50 min.	55 min.
Sch. F (1040): Cash Method	4 hr., 2 min.	34 min.	1 hr., 14 min.	20 min.
Sch. F. (1040): Accrual Method	4 hr., 22 min.	25 min.	1 hr., 19 min.	20 min.
Sch. R (1040)	20 min.	15 min.	22 min.	35 min.
Sch. SE (1040): Short	20 min.	13 min.	10 min.	14 min.
Sch. SE (1040): Long	26 min.	22 min.	38 min.	20 min.

Source: Internal Revenue Service, 1993 *1040 Forms and Instructions.*

8606, 8822, and 8829. If you don't need these forms, better you should remain ignorant of them.) A full accounting would require detailed knowledge of every tax form, how many of each schedule were attached, and how much estimated time each schedule requires. Nor have we yet mentioned business taxpayers, who must cope with a much heavier reporting burden.

To the arithmetic. The IRS estimates that the average total time to complete and file Form 1040A is six hours, thirty-three minutes. The time expands appreciably when it is necessary to attach any of Schedules 1 (Interest and Dividend Income), 2 (Child and Dependent Care Expenses), and 3 (Credit for the Elderly or Disabled) or any of the forms for EIC (earned income credit), IRA (individual retirement account) distributions, pension income, or Social Security benefits, so a reasonable average time is probably about eight hours. The time for Form 1040EZ is one hour, fifty-two minutes.

Few people treat filing tax returns as leisure activity; most people we know would rather fish, ski, or watch television. So we need to make some assumptions about the value of the time individuals expend complying with taxes.

For those who file Forms 1040EZ and 1040A, we use a conservative figure—the federal minimum wage of $4.35 an hour. For those who file Form 1040, we use the average hourly earnings in private, nonagricultural industry of about $10.80. These numbers are well below IRS costs of $21 an hour to process tax-related information back in 1985, which would be much higher today, or Arthur Andersen's employee cost of $35 an hour, again from 1985.

For those who file Form 1040EZ: 19.1 million taxpayers times one hour, fifty-two minutes, times $4.35 an hour totals $155 million. For filers of Form 1040A: 28.9 million taxpayers times eight hours times $4.35 an hour totals exactly $1 billion.

For filers of Form 1040, the calculations require a rough estimate of the average time per return. To be conservative, we will add up the times shown in IRS Form 1040 (minus any double counting) and add an additional 50 percent to include forms not listed (the depreciation form alone amounts to another forty-six hours). Our arithmetic sums to about 45.0 hours, which we adjust up to 67.5 hours for unlisted forms. Adding up: 65.7 million taxpayers times 67.5 hours times $10.80 an hour equals almost $48 billion. Altogether, compliance costs for individuals in 1993, at reasonable estimates, amounted to about $50 billion. Arthur Little's 1985 estimate was $51 billion, derived from 1.8 billion hours of work at an average cost of $28 an hour. (In 1985, eleven million fewer returns were filed compared with 1992. Also, the 1990 and 1993 tax increases significantly increased reporting requirements.) Our number, therefore, is extremely conservative.

The Arthur D. Little study concluded that twice as many hours were spent complying with business tax returns. It used a figure of $28.31 as the hourly tax compliance cost for business taxpayers in 1985. The arithmetic sums to $102 billion in business tax compliance costs in 1985. The Little study included commercial tax preparation charges in its estimate of business taxpayer costs. (However, it did not include the costs of tax planning.) Even half of Little's business compliance cost estimate, without any adjustment for inflation or an increase in the number of business firms in the United States, amounts to more than $50 billion. Any fair estimate of individual and business compliance costs must result in a twelve-digit number, more than $100 billion.

It's painful to add in the other costs of compliance. They include audits and correspondence, litigation, forced collections, and the unquantifiable emotional costs of coercion, especially in the face of high error rates in IRS proceedings.

Every year, the IRS undertakes more than one million audits, which are heavily focused on high-income taxpayers and large corporations. The cost to taxpayers of office, field, and mail audits easily exceeds $1 billion, with assessed penalties another $2 billion. The IRS's own annual reports admit a high rate of errors, and the IRS telephone information service gives out wrong answers as much as one-third of the time. A General Accounting Office study of the IRS's business nonfiler program found an error rate of 75 percent. Keep in mind that the government does not bear the cost of its errors; they are shifted onto taxpayers who must defend themselves against IRS mistakes. Payne documents more than a dozen government investigations of IRS mistakes. The important numerical finding is that the private-sector burden of initial enforcement contacts is higher than the total budget of the IRS. Here the taxpayer pays twice: once, to pay IRS salaries and overhead, second, to defend himself from the IRS. Estimates of tax litigation stemming from IRS contacts are again in the multibillion dollar range.

To be fair, the IRS is responsible for ensuring compliance with the tax code. Those who make mistakes or deliberately misreport income and deductions should be required to meet their lawful tax obligations. Therefore, a portion of these compliance costs is a legitimate burden of taxpayers. The difficulty arises from the complexity of the tax code. It's easy to make mistakes, even when taxpayers purchase electronic tax preparation programs. In addition, frustrated taxpayers are not likely to take extreme care with each of the hundreds of entries in as many as a dozen or more forms. Nor are taxpayers happy with high marginal rates, reaching over 40 percent, that result in the government taking a huge share of the fruits of their work. A simple system of low tax rates would remedy a good part of this.

The studies of compliance summarized in Payne's book were completed before the advent of computer software that permits taxpayers to record and save tax-related information throughout the year and that speeds up the entry and calculation of figures and the printing of final returns. No one has yet estimated how much time is saved from the use of tax preparation computer programs. It may be considerable. But some of these savings are offset by the purchase price of the software.

On balance, we think it fair to estimate compliance costs imposed on individuals and businesses at a minimum of $100 billion but probably higher.

INDIRECT COSTS

Estimating the indirect costs of the federal income tax is a more challenging proposition than adding up direct compliance costs, because indirect costs, by their very nature, are not precisely knowable. Who can estimate how many businesses were not formed because of high tax rates and elaborate reporting burdens? Who can estimate how many owners were unwilling to expand their business activities? Who really knows the size of the underground economy? Who can compute how much larger the economy would be if every dollar invested in a tax shelter went into productive investment? Who can predict how many wives, husbands, or others might enter or leave the work force with each rise or fall in tax rates? How many entrepreneurs have really been discouraged because of unnecessary capital gains taxes? In short, what would the American economy look like if the current complicated, multiple-bracket, high-rate tax system were scrapped in favor of a low, simple flat tax?

These and related topics have increasingly come under the scrutiny of economists, lawyers, and even the IRS. We propose to make a pass at the total by relying, again, on the best available scholarly evidence.

The first component of these lost economic benefits could be called *disincentive costs*. A proper understanding of disincentive costs first requires some additional description of the current income tax. The federal income tax consists of two separate taxes: the corporation tax and the personal income tax. The two are not integrated (as they are in many countries). But it is important to understand, in a conceptual sense, that corporations do not pay taxes. Rather, corporations are convenient legal devices that earn income and pay taxes on behalf of their shareholders. When a corporation files its annual income tax return, it pays profits tax on behalf of the firm's owners. But when the firm pays its shareholders dividends from its after-tax profits, the same stream of income is then subject to double taxation. The effective tax rate is the sum of the corporate tax rate plus the individual tax rate on ordinary income multiplied by the amount of dividends paid out plus the individual capital gains rate multiplied by the retained earnings. The retained funds increase the value of the shares and so generate capital gains. When the federal government taxes capital gains, it also constitutes double taxation of the same stream of income.

Moreover, under the current tax system, interest is deductible. This means that firms have an incentive to borrow, and deduct the costs, and a disincentive to issue equity because returns on equity are double taxed. This is not a healthy way to run a corporate sector.

Any increase in personal tax rates has a doubly pernicious effect because it simultaneously reduces returns from investment in ownership of the thousands of firms that trade on all the country's stock exchanges.

Since the 1970s, a number of prominent economists have attempted to identify the disincentive costs associated with taxation. The list includes Charles L. Ballard, Michael J. Boskin, Edgar K. Browning, Roger H. Gordon, Jane G. Gravelle, Arnold Harberger, Jerry A. Hausman, Dale W. Jorgenson, Laurence J. Kotlikoff,

Burton G. Malkiel, John Shoven, Charles E. Stuart, John Whalley, and Kun-Young Yun. Some tried to estimate the disincentive cost of taxation on labor, when people stop working or work less, some on capital gains, when people stop saving or investing, some on corporate formation and growth, when new firms are not established or when existing firms do not expand, and some on all federal taxation, which affects all forms of economic activity.

Most of these studies try to estimate the cost of raising one additional dollar of taxes from the existing tax level and system, in other words, how much lost output in terms of labor supply, capital supply, or total output is due to each new dollar of taxes. As expected, results vary widely. First, scholars study different taxes. Second, they use different models. Third, they make different assumptions about how those who supply capital, entrepreneurship, or labor will respond. The studies identify disincentive costs, as a percentage of taxes collected, that range from a low of 24 percent (taxes on labor) to an astonishing 151 percent (on the corporate income tax). Two studies that attempt to estimate the disincentive costs of all federal taxes, including Social Security, calculate a range of 33 to 46 percent of total federal taxes.

It's hard to translate these results into dollars because these studies try to estimate the disincentive costs of additional taxes imposed on the current system, not the total disincentive costs of the entire tax system or any part of the tax system. We try to get a better handle on total costs in the paragraphs that follow; for now, we want to observe that every scholarly study on this subject concludes that there are strong disincentive costs associated with the current tax system. No one says that collecting taxes is cost-free to the economy. Every time the federal government takes one more dollar in taxes from private hands, it discourages another thirty cents of additional output.

Let's apply the conservative finding of 30 percent of disincentive costs associated with new taxation to the current system. In 1990 President Bush signed legislation designed to raise about $250 billion in new taxes over five years. President Clinton repeated the exercise in 1993. On the 30 percent disincentive cost formula, the two tax increases will cost the economy $150 billion in lost output, which is considerably larger than total corporate income taxes. It is more than all federal health expenditures. It is larger than total Medicare outlays. It's within hailing range of annual federal interest outlays to service the national debt.

Looked at in this way, the $500 billion in new taxes amounts to a total tax increase of $650 billion on the American economy. The truth, however, is that government collections of new taxes rarely meet projections. The reason is that taxpayers are not docile sheep. Rather, most are clever, enterprising managers of their own personal affairs, quick to take advantage of legal ways to reduce taxes, known as tax avoidance or shelters, while some are inclined to cheat after every new tax increase. This takes us to our next segment.

Tax Evasion

Tax evasion is a polite term for cheating, the failure to pay what the tax law requires. The IRS, which has studied tax evasion for a long time, relies on a periodic, indepth tax audit known as the Taxpayer Compliance Measurement Program, TCMP, to estimate how much is owed but not collected in taxes. The TCMP breaks down unpaid taxes into the "legal sector tax gap" and the "illegal sector tax gap." Failure to pay taxes on lawful activity constitutes about 90 percent of unpaid taxes, despite the high level of publicity for tax cheating on income from illegal drugs, gambling, prostitution, and other illicit activities. Most unpaid taxes stem from dishonest reporting of honest activity.

How large is the figure and what are the chief causes of tax evasion? IRS estimates range from about $60 billion in 1973 to $76 billion in 1981 to well over $100 billion in the mid to late 1980s. In May 1994, the General Accounting Office, the U.S. government's watchdog agency, reported that the IRS failed to collect $127 billion in taxes in 1992, about 18 percent of what taxpayers owed. What are the main sources of cheating? In order of importance, they are underreporting income (about 70 percent), overstating deductions (17 percent), failing to pay obligations (9 percent), and failing to file (4 percent). If correct, these numbers are so large that the federal budget would have been in balance throughout the 1970s and 1980s if the tax code had collected every penny lawfully owed to the government. Given the prominence that some politicians attach to deficit reduction, reforming the federal income tax as a means to reduce the deficit makes more sense than adding new and more-complicated levies to the current system.

In 1983 the American Bar Association (ABA) formed a Commission on Taxpayer Compliance, consisting of lawyers (including past IRS commissioners), certified public accountants, social scientists (including Rabushka), and business executives. In July 1987, the commission published its findings on the causes of "tax gap" and how to close it. We quote from page 8 of the report: "Explanations of individual noncompliance frequently focus on high tax rates, the perceived unfairness of the tax system and the complexity of compliance."

We have so far discussed the complexity and costs of compliance; in chapter 2 we turn to "unfairness" and the consequences of high tax rates. The commission warned that the moral fabric that sustains our tax system, one of voluntary tax assessment and reporting, is fraying badly, meaning that citizens are increasingly willing to condone tax cheating among friends, relatives, and business associates.

The commission also minced no words about the benefits of reducing tax rates. It stated that "the Tax Reform Act of 1986, by sharply decreasing marginal tax rates and eliminating many tax preferences, should help to undercut many of the common justifications for tax cheating." As noted at the outset of this chapter, the 1986 act barely lasted out the decade. The 1990 and 1993 tax increases have restored the common justifications for tax cheating by increasing rates and creating new preferences.

To summarize, the perceived unfairness of complex and high tax rates deprives the IRS of more than $100 billion in lawfully owed taxes. This means that a fair, simple, low-rate tax system would collect far more in taxes than the current complex, high-rate system. The best remedy for future deficit reduction lies in replacing the current code with a simple, low-rate system, not in imposing new or higher taxes. In chapter 3 we make the case for the flat tax.

Taxpayers should not believe that Congress has their interests at heart. In late September 1994, Congress approved an additional $2 billion over the next five years for the Internal Revenue Service to "crack down on tax cheats." The U.S. government believes that more money spent on enforcement would collect an additional $9.2 billion in revenue. Perhaps someday the government will recognize that lower tax rates are a better solution to taxpayer compliance than stricter enforcement.

We should be clear on one point. The billions that are not paid in taxes, which stay in the hands of taxpayers, add to private welfare. Tax cheating may mean that the federal government has to borrow more than it would like to balance its books, but it doesn't necessarily make the individuals who cheat substantially worse off. The economy as a whole, and all of its participants, however, would be better off if federal borrowing were substantially reduced or eliminated—especially if a balanced budget stemmed from the greater efficiency of a low, simple flat tax rather than from an increase in tax rates or new taxes. In addition, there is a large social cost from turning a nation of generally honest residents into criminals, as recognized in the ABA report. If residents won't obey the tax laws, it becomes much easier to disregard other forms of lawful authority. This cannot be healthy in the long run.

Tax Avoidance

Tax avoidance does not sound nice, but it is perfectly legal. The basic concept is to keep taxes as low as possible by taking advantage of every conceivable technicality in the tax law. Sometimes the line between tax evasion and tax avoidance becomes blurred, which is why many taxpayers pay fancy fees to lawyers and accountants to ensure that aggressive tax avoidance does not result in criminal charges for tax evasion.

The terminology of tax avoidance is extensive. We are all vaguely familiar with such words as *loopholes, tax shelters, tax expenditures, tax credits, exemptions, deductions, allowances*, and the like. How many opportunities exist in the federal income tax code to shelter income from taxation? The list appears in Special Appendix G, Tax Expenditures, in each year's federal budget. A tax expenditure is the government's estimate of the amount of money taxpayers would have paid into the IRS if specific items were not exempted from taxation. The number of such items rose from a relatively meager 50 in 1967 to 104 in 1981, and the estimate of lost tax revenues rose from $37 billion to $229 billion. By 1986, the figure had reached $500 billion.

One popular loophole, or tax shelter, is the deduction for property taxes. Another is making gifts of appreciated stock to charities, whereby the market value can be written off against current income.

These common approaches to tax avoidance, which try to reduce taxes by taking advantage of specific deductions, are only part of the story. Most people don't even think of everyday deductions as tax avoidance. They believe that they are entitled to every category listed on Schedule A (Itemized Deductions) and on other forms, such as Schedule C (Profit or Loss from Business) and Form 4562 (Depreciation and Amortization).

What is the total value of all tax expenditures, or loopholes? In 1986, before the passage of the Tax Reform Act of 1986, tax expenditures totaled about $500 billion. In 1989, this number fell to about $400 billion. In part, the 1986 act closed certain loopholes, thereby eliminating some opportunities for tax avoidance. But the rate reduction in 1986, from a top bracket of 50 to 28 percent, meant that the total value of any deduction, such as home mortgage interest, was worth less. Whereas those in the top bracket received a tax refund of fifty cents on every dollar of mortgage interest deduction in 1985, that refund fell to twenty-eight cents after 1986. Lower rates, by themselves, reduce the total amount of tax avoidance.

Tax expenditures are back above $500 billion. Higher tax rates on upper-income households have increased the value of all deductions and other tax benefits. At the same time, many tax shelters that were not worth getting into at a 28 percent top tax rate are again

attractive at top rates above 40 percent. Recent history
suggests that the most constructive way to reduce or
eliminate tax avoidance is to reduce tax rates to low
levels, which encourages individuals to focus on productive work or investment rather than tax reduction
measures.

Let's try to put a number on tax avoidance. We
know that tens of billions of dollars flow into economic
activities that receive preferential treatment from the tax
code. If that money was entirely invested in productive
economic activity, it would generate billions more in
additional output.

Tax avoidance is a costly business to the U.S. economy. Some of the country's best minds in the legal and
accounting professions work around the clock searching
for loopholes in the tax regulations. Then they put together investment vehicles to exploit these loopholes,
spend time and money to market tax-advantaged investment opportunities to potential investors, and finally stay
on guard to fend off IRS challenges. None of this is
productive activity in the sense of creating anything of
value to society. Its sole objective is to help some taxpayers pay less in taxes. The real cost is the goods and
services these talented people would have supplied if
their lives were not devoted to mining the tax system,
along with a better allocation of investment dollars to
genuinely productive activities.

Sheltering income is a major industry. Tax lawyers
number some 50,000 to 100,000; accountants who
worry about tax-related issues number 100,000 to
200,000, and sellers of tax-advantaged investments sur-

pass 100,000. Tax planning has become a respected profession. A reasonable estimate is that as many as half a million people earn part or all of their living from helping taxpayers cope with, or take advantage of, the tax code. Using a conservative average figure of $75,000 as annual income for members of the tax avoidance profession, taxpayers shell out as much as $35 billion to support this industry.

Together we have presented our flat-tax plan on more than a thousand occasions since 1981. Jokingly, the most frequently asked question is how the country would cope with the white-collar recession that massive simplification of the tax code would create, throwing as many as 500,000 people out of work, not to mention the tens of thousands of part-timers who aid H & R Block and other tax preparation firms during tax-filing season.

There is another, often overlooked, cost of the current system. Businesses and individuals spend money and effort to influence Congress. The system of high rates coupled with hundreds of loopholes encourages factions to lobby for preferential treatment for themselves while persuading Congress to force other groups to pay more in taxes. But every group behaves this way. Overall, the economy is the loser, as more and more economic activities come under the sway of the tax system, either receiving special benefits or bearing disproportionate costs. A low flat tax on all income, to anticipate our argument, would eliminate this political game. It is an astonishing fact that there are more attorneys in Washington, D.C., than in New York City, whose population is triple that of the capital. Moreover, few attorneys in the capital practice law as we know it; most work at lobbying Congress and the executive branch. James Madison, who warned of the deleterious political effects of factions in *The Federalist* papers, probably regrets not having written a low flat tax into the U.S. Constitution.

Total Costs

It's time to sum the figures. Direct compliance costs, both in filing and in buying expert advice, exceed $100 billion. Direct tax-planning costs—consulting with lawyers, accountants, purveyors of tax shelters, and financial planners—exceed $35 billion. Revenue lost to the Treasury due to evasion exceeds $100 billion. Distortions from pursuing tax-advantaged investments in the form of lost output may exceed $100 billion. Finally, the lobbyists who inhabit Washington's K Street corridor probably cost the economy more than $50 billion. Total individual and corporate income taxes for the 1993 fiscal year (October 1, 1992—September 30, 1993) were about $625 billion. How politicians of both parties have been able to enact two major tax increases since 1990, supposedly to reduce future deficits, without first undertaking a complete reform of the current system must constitute one of the greatest political crimes of modern American history!

A BRIEF HISTORY OF THE
FEDERAL INCOME TAX

Two facts are paramount in understanding the present tax system. First, until the Great Depression of the 1930s, Americans held to the notion of a limited role for the federal government and correspondingly low taxes. In 1929, the federal government spent about 3 percent of the gross national product. (In sharp contrast, it spent almost 24 percent in 1993, an eightfold increase.) Save for periods of war or recession, revenues from customs and excises were sufficient to fund those activities widely regarded as proper federal functions. Excise taxes on domestic manufactured products and duties on imported coffee, tea, iron, cotton, and woolen goods provided the bulk of federal revenue.

Periods of war or recession, which strain federal finances, have led the government to seek additional sources of revenue. The Civil War, which produced an immediate need for new sources of funding, gave birth to the first American income tax. Enacted in 1861, it granted a $600 exemption and imposed a 3 percent charge on incomes below $10,000 and 5 percent on incomes above that level. The tax rates were increased to range from 5 to 10 percent in 1864. Receipts from this tax peaked in 1866, accounting for about 25 percent of federal revenue. The tax was allowed to lapse in 1872 on the grounds that it was an invasion of privacy and had a "socialistic tendency."

Note three important features of the first U.S. income tax. Despite its prominence as a source of wartime finance, the exemption of $600 meant that poor and middle-class households paid no income taxes; only wealthy persons paid what was a highly progressive levy. Second, the top rate never exceeded 10 percent. Third, a modest income tax could generate large amounts of money. *The first U.S. income tax was a low, simple tax, with a large exemption.*

Members of Congress did not forget the chief lesson of the temporary Civil War income tax—its capacity to generate huge amounts of revenue. Between 1873 and 1893, they introduced, in vain, sixty-eight different income tax bills, ostensibly to reform and reduce federal tariffs but also to collect more money. Finally, in 1894, a 2 percent income tax on incomes over $4,000 was attached to a tariff bill, which, after considerable controversy, became law. But, on a five-to-four vote, the U.S. Supreme Court declared the tax unconstitutional and in violation of Article 1, Section 2, paragraph 3, which says that all direct taxes must be levied among the states in proportion to their population.

Congress persisted. To circumvent the Supreme Court, it proposed the now famous Sixteenth Amendment on July 12, 1909, which was ratified by the states on February 29, 1913. It authorized Congress to tax incomes "from whatever source derived, without apportionment among the several States, and without regard to any census or enumeration." That year Congress enacted the first legal income tax, which provided a $3,000 exemption for single persons and $4,000 for married couples. The tax rate structure began at 1 percent on the first $20,000 of taxable income. It imposed six "super tax" brackets of 1 percent each on additional chunks of taxable income, reaching a top rate of 7 percent on taxable income over $500,000. Corporate profits were taxed at a standard rate of 1 percent without provision for a surtax.

This first lawful federal income tax was truly the thin edge of the wedge. Only 0.4 percent of the population filed tax returns in 1913. The personal exemptions eliminated more than 99 percent of all individuals from the tax net. To put this tax in perspective, federal tax receipts in 1913 amounted to only 2.6 percent of the gross national product.

During congressional debate on the Sixteenth Amendment, proponents promised that the top rate could never conceivably surpass 10 percent. This "read my lips" pledge is one of the shortest-lived promises in U.S. tax history. The outbreak of World War I in 1914 led Congress to amend, almost overnight, the 1913 federal income tax. First, it reduced the large exemptions for single persons and married couples, thus extending the tax to one-fifth of the adult population. The income tax was transformed from a tax on the wealthy to a tax on the burgeoning middle class. Second, it raised the bottom rate from 1 to 6 percent, which previously only the wealthiest of the wealthy paid, and raised the top bracket from 7 to 77 percent on taxable income over $1 million. Within five years of the ratification of the Sixteenth Amendment, the incipient federal income tax had shown its potential for what would become an insatiable congressional appetite for revenue.

But the times had not yet changed. During the

1920s, Secretary of the Treasury Andrew Mellon reduced the top rate from 77 to 25 percent even as total revenues, adjusted for inflation, increased 3 percent. Despite an apparent windfall to the rich, the system in fact became more progressive, that is, high-income taxpayers paid a greater fraction of total taxes than before. In 1921, taxpayers with incomes over $100,000 paid 28 percent of total income tax revenues; in 1926, they paid 51 percent. Those at the bottom, with incomes less than $10,000, paid 23 percent in 1921, declining to 5 percent in 1926. The main reason for the shift in the tax burden is that formerly high-bracket taxpayers shifted assets from tax-free bonds into productive outlets.

President Herbert Hoover could not leave well enough alone. The Great Depression slowed U.S. economic activity and reduced federal revenues. In pursuit of a balanced budget, President Hoover sponsored tax increases that raised the top bracket from 25 to 63 percent, while reducing personal exemptions. In the 1930s, the income tax became everyone's tax. With each reduction in personal exemptions, an ever-increasing share of the adult population was caught in the tax net.

World War II completed the transformation of what had once been a low, simple tax with a large personal exemption. The top bracket was increased to an astonishing 94 percent. This is as close to complete confiscation of personal income above a certain level as a tax system can get. The postwar Congress granted some relief to top-bracket taxpayers, lowering their rate from 94 to 85 percent. However, that relief was short-lived. Congress raised the top rate to 91 percent during the Korean War, where it remained until the early 1960s.

President John F. Kennedy introduced legislation that reduced the rate structure from a range of 20 to 91 percent to an across-the-board range of 14 to 70 percent. In 1969, Congress modified the income tax so as to limit the top marginal rate on wages and salaries to 50 percent. In 1981, Congress passed President Ronald Reagan's three-year, 25 percent, across-the-board reduction, which replaced the 14 to 70 percent range with an 11 to 50 percent range for all types of income.

President Reagan was not consistent in his approach to federal income taxation. He signed the Tax Equity and Fiscal Responsibility Act of 1982 (TEFRA 1982), which was designed to raise $98 billion over three years, followed by the Deficit Reduction Act of 1984, to raise more than $20 billion a year into the indefinite future.

In his second term, the president concentrated his political efforts on extending the rate reductions of the 1981 legislation. He succeeded with the Tax Reform Act of 1986, which, as previously noted, replaced the morass of multiple rates with two rates, 15 and 28 percent, and closed almost $100 billion in loopholes, thereby broadening the tax base. Although the 1986 act dramatically reduced marginal tax rates, especially on the top tax bracket, it did not cut total taxes, and, almost immediately, Congress set about increasing total taxes. It enacted the Omnibus Budget Reconciliation Act of 1987 (OBRA87) to generate more than $10 billion every year, the Omnibus Budget Reconciliation Act of 1990 (OBRA90), $250 billion in new taxes over five years, and the Omnibus Reconciliation Act of 1993 (OBRA93), $241 billion in additional federal revenues over five years. President Reagan's top marginal rate of 28 percent is now President Clinton's top rate of 39.6 percent, a 41 percent increase in the top tax bracket.

2. What's Fair about Taxes?

ECONOMISTS AND POLITICIANS of all persuasions agree on three points. One, the federal income tax is not simple. Two, the federal income tax is too costly. Three, the federal income tax is not fair. However, economists and politicians do not agree on a fourth point: What does fair mean when it comes to taxes? This disagreement explains, in large measure, why it so difficult to find a replacement for the federal income tax that meets the other goals of simplicity and low cost.

In recent years, the issue of fairness has come to overwhelm the other two standards used to evaluate tax systems: cost (efficiency) and simplicity. Recall the 1992 presidential campaign. Candidate Bill Clinton preached that those who "benefited unfairly" in the 1980s [the Tax Reform Act of 1986 reduced the top tax rate on upper-income taxpayers from 50 percent to 28 percent] should pay their "fair share" in the 1990s. What did he mean by such terms as "benefited unfairly" and should pay their "fair share?" Were the 1985 tax rates fair before they were reduced in 1986? Were the Carter 1980 tax rates even fairer before they were reduced by President Reagan in 1981? Were the Eisenhower tax rates fairer still before President Kennedy initiated their reduction? Were the original rates in the first 1913 federal income tax unfair? Were the high rates that prevailed during World Wars I and II fair? Were Andrew Mellon's tax rate cuts unfair? Are the higher tax rates President Clinton signed into law in 1993 the hallmark of a fair tax system, or do rates have to rise to the Carter or Eisenhower levels to be fair?

No aspect of federal income tax policy has been more controversial, or caused more misery, than allegations that some individuals and income groups don't pay their fair share. This is especially true when it comes to the flat tax, which has been a centerpiece of tax policy debate since 1981 and which has been introduced in almost every Congress since 1982. Few economists or politicians challenge the flat tax on grounds of simplicity or efficiency; rather, their critiques rest primarily on one emotionally laden charge: It would give a windfall to the rich and, therefore, is unfair to the poor and the middle class. Opponents of the flat tax claim that it shifts the tax burden from wealthier to lower- and middle-income households.

Few critics of the flat tax defend the current system as fair. It's hard to imagine that any reasonable person would describe as fair an incomprehensible, costly system that requires professional advice, costs taxpayers and the economy hundreds of billions of dollars, treats taxpayers with similar incomes in radically different ways, and puts taxpayers at a severe disadvantage in dealing with the IRS. An NBC News/*Wall Street Journal* poll conducted during July 23–26, 1994, asked the following question: "Do you think that the current income tax system is basically fair, or basically unfair?" Fifty-nine percent replied "basically unfair"; only 38 percent said it was "basically fair." Two-thirds of those who said it was unfair thought it could only be made fair with a complete overhaul, not with some minor adjustments. This pattern of response was roughly similar between men and women, whites and blacks, all main occupational groups, Democrats and Republicans, Bush and Clinton voters, and liberals and conservatives. Perot voters, political independents, and those without college degrees said it was unfair in higher percentages. The only majority that said it was fair were those sixty-five and over.

Because of the virtual consensus on the efficiency and simplicity of the flat tax, the debate about the merits of a flat tax boils down to, Can it be fair? Can it be at least as fair, or more fair, than the current system? Is it more or less fair than other proposals that try to reduce the costs and complexities of the current system?

A flat rate of taxation is not a novel idea. Flat rates are in wide use throughout the United States. The best example is the Social Security tax, which levies one uniform rate on all employees and the self-employed. All workers are subject to a uniform tax rate for Medicare. The sales tax rate is the same for all consumers, rich and poor alike. Property tax rates on assessed valuations of real property are the same for all homeowners. All these tax rates are proportional to income, purchases, or property values. In general, government licenses and fees for government services are fixed regardless of income or wealth. Except for income taxes, flat-rate taxes are in wide use by, and supply most of the revenues for, all levels of government in the United States.

This chapter makes three important points. First,

the flat tax is fair on the basis of historical and commonsense notions of fairness. Second, the flat tax is fair
based on who pays, especially when compared with the
current U.S. federal income tax system. Third, the flat
tax enjoys wide support from all sides of the political
spectrum and the media.

WHAT'S FAIR?

Are there any objective definitions or standards of fairness we can use to choose among tax systems? Is one
person's claim about what's fair just as valid as any
other's? How can we apply a standard of fairness unless
we know what it means?

Concepts of fairness can be found in popular, everyday usage as well as in formulations among lawyers,
economists, philosophers, and theologians. All these can
be found in the lengthy definitions found in most dic-
tionaries. Here are some of the definitions of the adjec-
tival use of *fair* that appear on pages 490 and 491 in the
third edition of Houghton Mifflin's 1993 *American Heritage College Dictionary*: 6.a. Having or exhibiting a dis-
position that is free of favoritism or bias; impartial; 6.b.
Just to all parties; equitable: *a fair deal*; 7. Being in
accordance with relative merit or significance: *her fair
share*; 8. Consistent with rules, logic, or ethics; 9. Mildly
good; mildly satisfying; 10. Superficially true or appeal-
ing; specious.

The idiom *fair and square* is defined as "just and
honest," while the idiom *no fair* means "something contrary to the rules." The list of synonyms further describes

what is meant by fair: *just, equitable, impartial, unprejudiced, unbiased, objective, dispassionate.* All these words mean free from favoritism, self-interest, or bias in general. The dictionary states that the word *fair* is the most general of these terms. "*Just* stresses conformity with what is legally or ethically right or proper." "*Equitable* implies justice dictated by reason, conscience, and a natural sense of what is fair to all concerned." The other terms mean "lack of favoritism, detachment that permits impersonal judgment, or free from strong emotions." On the last meaning, President Clinton's denunciation of the Tax Reform Act of 1986, charging that "the rich benefited unfairly in the 1980s," epitomizes the expression of strong emotions.

Some comments on these definitions: Number 10 fits much of the political discourse that mars the discussion of tax policy and contradicts numbers 6 through 8, which get at the commonsense notion of fair. Number 9 is so subjective and personal that it is of no use in choosing among tax systems. Numbers 6—8 best capture what most people take fair to mean: impartial, equitable, in accordance with merit or significance, and consistent with rules, logic, and evidence. In short, everyone should receive the same, or equal, treatment.

Taking stock, we cannot find anything in the etymologies or meanings of any of these words that says or implies that a flat rate of taxation is unfair or that a graduated, multiple-rate tax structure is more fair than a single rate. On the contrary, we would argue that the meanings of *even, just,* and *equal,* in keeping with rules and logic, better fit a flat rate of taxation than any multiple-rate system that discriminates among different classes of taxpayers.

When economists make judgments about fairness, they most often invoke the concept of equity. As it applies to taxation, and tax burdens in particular, equity has historically meant equal treatment of equals. This usage conforms to American constitutional guarantees of equal treatment before the law. To discriminate among equal classes of taxpayers is arbitrary, capricious, and generally regarded as wrong. In the dictionary senses listed above, discriminatory treatment is not just, impartial, or consistent with logic or a set of rules. So, for example, if two families earn identical incomes, the doctrine of equity implies that each should pay identical amounts in taxes.

In law, equity has a different, specific meaning. Here, *equity* refers to justice applied in circumstances covered by law yet influenced by principles of ethics and fairness, which serve to modify the rigor of common law. As applied to the example of two households with identical incomes, a wise tax system might want to reduce the tax burden of one family that incurred heavy medical expenditures, suffered the ravages of storm damage, or bore costs to move to a new job, compared with the other family that had no unusual expenditures. Applying different tax rates to the two families in similar circumstances, however, is an entirely different matter and would violate the norm of equity predicated on equal treatment under the law.

Economists use the term *horizontal equity* to mean that people under similar circumstances should bear equal tax burdens. As a general principle, a flat tax (also called a uniform, proportional, or single-rate tax) satisfies this norm. Even Harvard philosopher John Rawls, a fervent advocate of redistribution, concludes in his controversial book *A Theory of Justice* that "a proportional expenditure tax may be . . . the best tax scheme." The principle of equity embodied in the flat tax is that every taxpayer pays taxes in direct proportion to his income. As incomes double, triple, or grow tenfold, tax obligations double, triple, or rise tenfold. Those who earn more pay more.

In practice, the horizontal equity norm invariably includes a provision for exempting low-income families from income taxes. Today, this provision takes the form of a combination of personal exemptions and the standard deduction.

As recently as 1929, federal taxes from all sources amounted to a modest 3 percent of the gross national product (GNP). Since the end of the Korean War, federal taxes have averaged about 19 percent of GNP (regardless of the number of tax brackets and the level of the top marginal rate), a more than sixfold rise. Something dramatic happened during the years between the beginning of the Great Depression and the beginning of the New Deal to change the national political consensus on low taxation and limited government that prevailed during the first 175 years of our country's existence.

The dramatic growth in government went hand in hand with the belief that fiscal policy could be a tool for redistributing income. First, a huge increase in federal tax burdens was deemed essential to finance transfer payments and large government programs. Second, the imposition of steeply graduated tax rates was seen by many as a desirable way to achieve greater equality in the distribution of after-tax income. Those in charge of this intellectual and political transformation found a new norm of *vertical equity* with which to replace the former, established norm of horizontal equity. They called this new norm the *ability to pay*.

It is important to keep in mind that this new interpretation of equity, a redistributionist approach to achieving tax fairness, is not rooted in the philology of, or in traditional approaches to, fairness. The new approach, a twentieth-century phenomenon about a half century old, has come to mean that successful people, with above-average incomes, should have to pay higher fractions of their incomes in taxes. The penalty is imposed by applying a series of graduated tax rates in which additional chunks of income are taxed at steadily higher and higher rates. The 1993 tax bill, to illustrate the point, has five tax brackets. Married couples filing jointly pay 15 percent on the first $36,900 of taxable income, 28 percent on income between $36,900 and $89,150, 31 percent on the next $50,850 up to $140,000, 36 percent on the next $110,000 up to

$250,000, and 39.6 percent on all taxable income over $250,000.

Vertical equity does not fare well in practice. Despite attempts to equalize after-tax incomes through steeply graduated tax rates, one Congress after another has riddled the tax code with hundreds of loopholes that permit some millionaires to pay no income taxes whatsoever and some high earners to pay low taxes. Good examples are tax-free municipal bonds and charitable contributions. Other loopholes permit the wealthy to exploit tax shelters that reduce large incomes to modest levels of taxable income. One historian of the income tax, John Witte, has concluded that "there is no evidence that the income tax significantly redistributes income." The reason is that every time tax rates are increased, Congress, in response to political pressures from organized interest groups, inserts new deductions and loopholes into the tax code to offset the effects of higher rates. The ideology of vertical equity, or ability to pay, runs smack into the economic and political realities of economic distortions and well-organized interests.

More fundamentally, we believe that high tax rates abridge individual liberty in a free society. Politicians and intellectuals who support high tax rates to redistribute income to attain their egalitarian goals threaten individual freedom and self-reliance.

What is the correct amount of fairness based on the new doctrine of vertical equity? What share of total taxes should be borne by each income category? No one really seems to know, and the numbers change every few

years. Politicians and intellectuals have trouble making
up their minds on the right amount of fairness because
there is no objective standard and because fairness is
not cost-free. High tax rates reduce economic output.
They also foster tax avoidance and evasion (see chapter
1). Concern with the disincentive costs of high tax rates
has prompted successive presidents and Congresses to
reduce the top tax bracket from 92 percent in the 1950s
to 70 percent in the 1960s to 50 percent in the early
1980s to 28 percent in 1986. Each cut in the top bracket
moved the norm of fairness closer to its historical meaning of horizontal equity.

So far we've talked about taxes in simple, everyday
language. But some aspects of taxation are technical and
require precise terminology. It may be useful here, and
valuable in trying to understand the problems in the
current U.S. income tax code and the benefits of our
proposed flat-tax plan, to present concepts and definitions of tax jargon in ordinary English.

TERMINOLOGY OF TAXATION —
UNDERSTANDING TAXES

We begin with the *tax rate*. There are two notions of
tax rate: *average*, or effective, tax rate and *marginal* tax
rate. A taxpayer's average tax rate is the fraction of income paid in taxes. To calculate the average tax rate,
divide taxes paid by income. For example, $1,000 paid
in taxes on an income of $10,000 yields a 10 percent
average tax rate. The average tax rate is sometimes defined as the tax *level* or tax *burden*. These three terms

are often used interchangeably and can refer to one tax-payer, a group of taxpayers, or all taxpayers in the economy. The marginal tax rate, in contrast, applies to the last dollar earned. If the person earning $10,000 gets $11,000 and then pays $1,200 in taxes, the tax on the extra $1,000 is $200 and the marginal rate is 20 percent. The average rate in this example rises from 10 to 10.9 percent. To use other popular terminology, the person's tax burden amounts to 10.9 percent, but he faces a marginal rate of 20 percent on his last chunk of income. It this example, as in most tax systems, the marginal rate exceeds the average rate.

The U.S. individual income tax system contains five tax brackets, ranging from a low of 15 percent to a high of 39.6 percent. (In 1985, it contained fourteen brackets that ranged between 11 and 50 percent, while in 1987, it contained only two brackets, 15 and 28 percent.) As increases in income push people into higher tax brackets, a greater proportion of each additional dollar of income is paid in taxes. Someone paying a marginal tax rate of 15 percent gets to keep 85 cents of each additional dollar; at 28 percent, 72 cents are left. At the current top rate of 39.6 percent, 60.4 cents are left. Under current law, a family with a taxable income of $50,000 pays an average rate of 18 percent and faces a marginal rate of 28 percent. It is the top marginal rate, the tax on the last dollar earned, not the average rate (or tax burden), that sets incentives. The marginal rate determines whether the taxpayer decides to work overtime, search for a tax shelter, cheat on taxes, or go fishing.

The income tax has changed dramatically over time. Rates in the 1961 tax code ranged from 20 to 91 percent. However, 88 percent of all tax returns paid a marginal rate in the 20 to 22 percent category. Ten percent were in the 23 to 31 percent range, and only 2 percent exceeded 32 percent. For almost 90 percent of the taxpaying population, the 1961 tax code amounted to a 22 percent flat tax. By 1979, the picture was totally transformed: 45 percent of all taxpayers paid marginal tax rates of more than 23 percent. Millions of American taxpayers paid marginal rates that had been intended only for the very rich just two decades earlier.

What happened? Inflation pushed taxpayers into tax brackets with higher marginal rates, a phenomenon that is termed *bracket creep*. Even with no change in purchasing power (that is, the real purchasing power that remains after taxes and the effects of inflation are removed), taxpayers were pushed into ever-higher marginal tax brackets and their incentives were adversely affected.

The Economic Recovery Tax Act of 1981, recognizing the dangers of bracket creep, included a provision for indexing tax brackets, the personal exemption, and the standard deduction, or zero bracket, to offset the effects of inflation. Once indexing provisions were put in place, taxpayers would face higher tax brackets only when their real purchasing power increased.

Even without inflation, bracket creep is the effect of a *graduated tax rate structure*, which means that as a family's real income rises, it has to share an increasing fraction of each increment with the tax collector. Tax systems that aggressively try to redistribute income typically have heavily graduated rates. A graduated tax rate structure has the effect of cutting the government in on the growth of the economy, thereby transferring more and more of the national income into public hands, unless the government enacts tax reduction legislation—cutting rates or adding loopholes—to offset the trend. The dramatic rise in tax shelters, or what the government calls tax expenditures, in the 1970s was a direct consequence of the combined effect of inflation and graduated tax rates pushing taxpayers into higher brackets.

Indexing is a recent but not permanent feature of the income tax. Take the 1993 tax increase, for example. The new rates, reaching to 39.6 percent, took effect in the 1993 taxable year. However, the law provided that the two new brackets of 36 percent and 39.6 percent would not be indexed for inflation until after December 31, 1994, which meant that the 36 percent rate would affect taxpayers in the 1995 tax year at about $135,000 in real, inflation-adjusted 1993 dollars (compared with $140,000 stated in the law) and that the 39.6 percent rate would affect taxpayers in 1995 at about $240,000 in real 1993 dollars ($250,000 in the law). Inflation exceeding 4 percent would further exacerbate the impact of bracket creep. Moreover, it is possible that Congress will further postpone or completely suspend the indexing provision for the top two brackets. As evidence, previous changes in tax law introduced measures to phase out personal exemptions and up to 3 percent of itemized deductions above certain income levels but only through 1997. The 1993 tax law extends the phaseout provisions indefinitely.

It is important *not* to equate graduated rates with *progressivity*. A tax system is progressive when it takes an increasing share of a taxpayer's income as that person's income rises or, as we can now say, if the average tax rate rises with income. To illustrate, consider three families with incomes of $10,000, $20,000, and $30,000. Suppose the three families paid taxes of $500, $2,500, and $4,500, respectively. The first family thus pays 5 percent of its income in taxes, the second, 10 percent, and the third, 15 percent. Such payments would satisfy the definition of progressivity because families with larger incomes paid a higher share of their income in taxes than those with smaller incomes. But the tax rate is not graduated in this example—the marginal tax rate is 20 percent for all three families.

It is not necessary for a progressive tax system to have rising marginal rates. In chapter 3 we design a progressive system with one flat rate. The key is to provide each taxpayer with a personal allowance and to tax all income above that allowance at the one rate. The allowance constitutes a *threshold* of taxation: taxes are imposed on income above the threshold and exempted below the threshold. In fact, the current system, with its five graduated rates, may be regressive because it gives high-bracket taxpayers numerous opportunities for legal deductions that reduce their average rates below those of middle- or lower-middle-income families that cannot utilize them. One gift of art, for example, can completely wipe out all tax liabilities for a millionaire in any given year, a provision fought for and won by the art museums of America. The elite institutions—universities, art museums, dance troupes—that house vocal supporters of graduated tax rates remain the strongest supporters of unrestricted deductions for the rich who make gifts of art or appreciated stock *to them*. For the inhabitants of these institutions, fairness is no match for self-interest!

Any income tax requires a precise definition of income to know what is being taxed. Take gross domestic product (GDP), which is the most comprehensive measure of the annual value of goods and services produced by a nation. The *tax base* against which any structure of tax rates is applied is that portion of GDP that remains after all allowable deductions and exemptions have been removed. Those items that have been removed may take the forms of *exemptions* (usually an allowance for each member of a taxpaying household), *deductions* (special provisions in the law for mortgage interest, charitable contributions, the standard deduction for those with few itemized deductions, and so on), *exclusions* (moving expenses, retirement contributions), and *credits* (sums that can be credited against tax liabilities). Collectively, these four categories are known as *loopholes*, devices that allow taxpayers to reduce their taxes. They are also called *tax preference items* or *tax expenditures*, the equivalent of the taxes the government does not collect on those social or economic activities for which it may seek to influence behavior or is responding to interest group pressure; it is as if the government were paying taxpayers to conduct those activities.

The effect of loopholes is to *narrow the tax base*, which means that there is less income to tax. As documented in chapter 1, the federal government counted 50 tax expenditure items in 1967 that cost the IRS an estimated $37 billion in uncollected taxes. By 1981, the number of tax expenditures had grown to 104, with an estimated loss of $229 billion, a total that more than doubled to over $500 billion in foregone revenues in 1986. By 1989 the figure had fallen to about $400 billion, but by 1993 it again surpassed $500 billion. The effect of all these loopholes, demanded and obtained by special-interest groups, is that the tax base is in the neighborhood of half the GDP.

Chapter 1 described the harmful effects of *tax shelters*—investments designed to generate deductions to offset income rather than investments to produce goods and services that consumers want. Aggressive shelters attempt to provide deductions larger than the amount of money invested in them. Home ownership, the most common tax shelter, permits taxpayers to deduct mortgage interest and property taxes; these deductions encourage people to buy, not rent. Taxpayers with low marginal rates have smaller incentives to buy homes as tax shelters because they can claim only 15.0 cents in tax benefits from every dollar of mortgage interest, unlike those in the top bracket, who can claim 39.6 cents. In the current tax code, the richer you are, the larger the benefit, a curious feature of a structure of tax rates designed to make the rich pay their fair share.

Tax shelters are used to *avoid* taxes. *Tax avoidance*, which is perfectly legal, is simply taking advantage of opportunities created in law to give preference to certain kinds of expenditures or investments. The problem with tax avoidance (see chapter 1) is that higher tax rates prompt investors to be more concerned with the tax advantages of investing than with its economic benefits, which costs the economy billions of dollars in lost or misdirected output.

Tax evasion, a polite word for cheating, also rises in tandem with increases in marginal tax rates. *The underground economy*, in which people barter (exchange goods and services for other goods and services with no cash changing hands) or pay unreported cash for goods and services, is less efficient than the legal economy: barter is less likely to place goods and services in the hands of those most likely to value them, and illegal organizations cannot gain efficient scale and must spend resources avoiding detection. Moreover, as the underground economy grows, it reduces the tax base, thereby shifting the burden of taxes to those who fully report their income.

A technical term relating to the issues of fairness and fair share is the *distribution of the tax burden*, or *incidence* of taxation, which focuses on the tax burden, or the share of income paid in taxes, by different income groups. Most discussions of alternative tax proposals focus on how different categories of taxpayers—typically identified in deciles or quintiles as poor, low income, middle class, upper middle class, and rich—would gain or lose under rival plans.

Finally, a new tax system can raise additional revenue, maintain the same level of revenue as the current system, or reduce receipts. A *revenue-neutral* reform is one that leaves revenue unchanged. Some proponents of tax reform not only want to simplify the system and lower marginal rates but also want to shrink the size of government by lowering revenues. Other proponents of tax reform strive to raise revenues to balance the budget at current levels of spending. Our flat tax, presented in chapter 3, is a revenue-neutral replacement for the current federal individual and corporate income taxes. A revenue-neutral flat tax allows us to talk about the benefits of tax reform without becoming embroiled in such issues as the size of government (it's probably too intrusive in the economy), the budget deficit (it's probably not good), or the Social Security system (whose tax is earmarked to specific retirement benefits). These are all valid issues but are not the subject of this book.

TYPES OF TAXES — A LEXICON

The U.S. government gets almost all its revenue from income taxes and Social Security taxes, with a very small portion from miscellaneous excise taxes, duties, fees, and charges. The states and localities, which are outside the scope of this book, rely heavily on sales and property taxes in addition to state and local income taxes. Less familiar is the terminology of consumption taxes, value-added taxes (VAT), excise taxes, wealth taxes, corporate taxes, and a myriad of other special levies. To understand the intricacies of the tax system and take part in public discussion on reforming the federal income tax, it is necessary to examine the major categories of federal taxation.

In fiscal year 1993, the federal government collected more than $1.1 trillion from the following sources: individual income tax (45 percent), social insurance taxes (38 percent), corporate income tax (9 percent), and excise taxes (4 percent), with the balance from estate and gift taxes, customs duties, and other miscellaneous items. (The exact percentages vary slightly from year to year; for example, corporate taxes vary with profitability.)

Sticking with 1993 for the moment, any proposal to replace the individual income tax would have to generate slightly more than $500 billion; any package that scrapped both the individual and corporate taxes would have to yield more than $600 billion. The plan set forth in chapter 3 is constructed to replace both individual and corporate taxes; it does not eliminate or replace social insurance, excises, customs, and other federal receipts. It is possible, of course, to do so, with a simple change in the tax rate. But the issue of the Social Security system is so large that, in our opinion, it requires separate treatment. It can happily coexist, however, with our simple flat tax.

Individual Income Tax

Although nearly everyone comes into contact with the federal income tax, it is nonetheless useful to describe its main features. Basically, taxpayers add up their income from all taxable sources, subtract certain allowable deductions and exemptions for themselves, spouses, and dependents, and then apply a table of taxes or schedule of tax rates to the balance. The two main concepts that convert income into taxes are *adjusted gross income* and *taxable income*. Adjusted gross income is a close approximation in the tax law to the economic or ordinary notion of total income, excluding moving expenses, retirement plan contributions, and a few special deductions. The tax code exempts some forms of income as taxable for a variety of social, economic, or political reasons: interest on state and municipal bonds, welfare payments, food stamps, fringe benefits, and other transfer payments.

To arrive at taxable income, the law permits a wide variety of deductions to be subtracted from adjusted gross income. Among the most popular are home mortgage interest, charitable contributions, some state and local government taxes, excessive medical expenses, casualty losses, and unreimbursed business expenses. Or one can take a standard deduction in place of an itemized list. Taxpayers are also allowed one or more personal exemptions, depending on family size. The combination of personal exemptions and deductions constitutes the threshold of taxable income. High thresholds increase progressivity.

According to the national income accounts, total personal income in 1992 was about $5 trillion. In its spring 1994 *Statistics of Income Bulletin*, the IRS released a preliminary analysis of individual income tax returns for 1992 (which excludes corporate returns). Total adjusted gross income was $3.64 trillion (about 73 percent of personal income). Taxable income was $2.4 trillion (slightly less than half of personal income), and total individual income taxes were $476 billion (about 9.5 percent of personal income). The base of taxable income is not quite half the total amount of personal income received by individuals, a ratio that has remained steady for more than a decade.

Which items contributed most to the shrinking tax base for individual income tax? Total itemized deductions were $487 billion; the three largest were home mortgage interest, $194 billion, state and local taxes, $159 billion, and charitable contributions, $63 billion. The value of standard deductions was $368 billion. Total deductions were $843 billion. Personal exemptions contributed another $525 billion.

IRS data reveal some interesting patterns. In 1992, taxpayers reported $29 billion rental net income but $29 billion rental net losses, exactly canceling each other out. More alarming is farming, which generated $10.5 billion net income and $12.2 billion net losses. The IRS would come out ahead if farming were exempted from taxation.

For readers interested in the main sources of adjusted gross income, salaries and wages provided 77 percent; taxable interest, 4 percent; business (excluding corporations) net income, 4 percent; capital gains, 3 percent; partnership and S Corporation net income, just over 2 percent; dividends, 2 percent; and Social Security benefits, less than 1 percent. Other items include pensions, unemployment compensation, and estates or trusts. These numbers mean that the bulk of all individual income taxes comes from wages and salaries, reflecting that three-quarters of the gross domestic product is paid to labor.

With the passage of the 1993 tax increases, a series of five rates, from 15.0 percent on the lowest bracket to 39.6 percent on the highest bracket, are applied to taxable income. The rate schedule is different for single people, married people filing separate returns, married couples filing joint returns, and heads of households. For a married couple filing jointly in 1993, the standard deduction was $6,200 and each personal exemption was $3,250. A family of four thus received $15,600 in tax benefits, meaning that it paid fifteen cents in tax on its first dollar of adjusted gross income exceeding $15,600, or taxable income is adjusted gross income minus $15,600.

Pages and pages of tax tables simplify computing tax up to a taxable income of $100,000. Others have to use the tax rate schedules. Schedule Y-1, for married filing jointly, charges 15 percent on taxable income (amount on Form 1040, line 37) up to $36,900; thereafter, 28 percent up to $89,150; 31 percent up to $140,000; 36 percent up to $250,000; and, 39.6 percent over $250,000. However, it's not that simple.

The income tax provides for phaseouts of personal exemptions and a portion of itemized deductions for upper-income taxpayers. Personal exemptions are phased out over adjusted gross incomes of $108,450 to $230,950 for single individuals and $162,700 to $285,000 for married couples filing jointly. Three percent of the value of itemized deductions is gradually lost on adjusted gross incomes above $108,450 for all filers, without an upper limit. These phaseouts effectively raise the top marginal rates for persons caught in these ranges.

Corporate Income Tax

Since 1981, the corporate income tax has generated, on average, about a fifth as much revenue as the individual income tax. But, unlike the individual income tax, it is hard to determine who pays the corporate tax.

It is important to distinguish between the *mechanics* of the corporate income tax and the *incidence* of it, that is, who really pays it. The first point is straightforward. Each year, every corporation files a corporate income tax return. The corporate tax is a tax on business, with deductions confined to expenses incurred doing business. To arrive at its business net income, a firm subtracts depreciation of capital, wages, pension contributions, goods and services purchased, interest paid, and a raft of special provisions too complicated to discuss here from gross receipts. The tax is extremely complicated; depreciation schedules that vary by item and a variety of methods can be used to calculate allowable depreciation. The rate structure applied to net income is mildly graduated, beginning at 15 percent of the first $50,000 of taxable income, rising to 25 percent on the next $25,000, and reaching a standard rate of 34 percent on income over $75,000. (A blip in the code applies a 39 percent rate to taxable income between $100,000 and $335,000, above which the 34 percent rate again takes hold.) The 1993 tax increase imposed a 35 percent rate on income over $10 million, 38 percent between $15 — 18.3 million, reverting to 35 percent over $18.3 million. Over half of corporate taxable income is subject to the top rate.

But one should not think of the corporate income tax as a tax on some anonymous entity. Rather, it is a tax on the individuals who, taken together, own a corporation. In this sense, the corporation is simply a collection device by which the IRS taxes the income of the owners of the business. To say that corporations do not pay their fair share in taxes can only mean that owners of corporations should pay higher taxes on income earned by corporate business entities.

So why do we have corporations if they serve largely to make the job of the IRS easier? The reason is that the corporation is a legal entity that provides special privileges and benefits to its owners (limited liability of shareholders, perpetual life, marketability of shares, growth through retention of earnings, and so forth). It is more suitable for conducting certain kinds of business than are sole proprietorships or partnerships.

Although it appears that the corporate income tax is collected from the owners of the business, economists disagree on whether its true incidence lies with stockholders, owners of capital through depressed rates of return, consumers through higher prices, workers in the form of lower wages, or some combination of these groups. A good illustration of this issue is the 1990 tax increase that imposed a 10 percent luxury tax on yachts. Although the measure increased the sales tax, not the corporate income tax, the principle is the same. The tax was repealed in 1993. Potential boat buyers, unwilling to pay the additional luxury tax, postponed new purchases of yachts. By raising the price of yachts, the tax reduced demand, a predictable result following the law of demand, the most basic principle of elementary economics. Fewer sales forced layoffs and lower wages. The 10 percent luxury tax on yachts was borne largely by laid-off yacht workers. Unemployed yacht builders were not impressed with the attempt to make the rich pay more.

The Problem of Double Taxation

An important feature of the corporate income tax is that, in conjunction with the individual income tax, it causes *double taxation*. Corporations pay dividends to shareholders *after* they pay taxes on business profits (with unknown incidence) at a 35 percent rate. Individuals, in addition to reporting wages and salaries, must declare dividends on their tax returns and pay taxes at rates up to 39.6 percent. Top-bracket taxpayers pay 39.6 percent on the 65 percent of corporate profits they receive in the form of dividends, assuming all business income is paid out in the form of dividends. (The incidence of tax on dividends is reported in IRS summaries of adjusted gross income from individual tax returns.) The combined tax on business income for an individual in the 39.6 percent bracket comes to 60.7 percent. Rates at this level impose heavy disincentives on entrepreneurial activities.

The problem of double taxation has generated numerous proposals to integrate corporate and individual income taxes. For example, companies might deduct dividends in computing corporate taxes. Or, more simply, dividends could be excluded from individuals' tax returns. Numerous countries around the world follow one of these two practices.

The corporate income tax in the United States has the peculiar property of imposing heavy tax rates and generating little revenue. Some economists maintain that the effective rate of taxation of corporations is low and thus we need not be concerned with any adverse effects of its statutory 35 percent rate or the purported effects of double taxation. Other economists maintain that the corporate tax is a major obstacle to growth, capital formation, and efficiency. We will not try to settle the issue. Rather, we will stress the shortcomings of the corporate tax in extracting revenue from business income and the adverse effects of its high tax rates.

Who Pays the Income Tax?

The income tax consists of payments to the IRS from individuals and corporations. It's easy to quantify payments from individuals, based on wages, dividends, interest, and a variety of other sources and activities, and subject them to analysis on the basis of age, sex, race, income category, region, and so forth. We cannot, unfortunately, do the same for corporate tax payments. Any serious attempt to determine tax burdens by income categories must take a stab at allocating that part of corporate income to individuals not paid out in dividends and corporate tax payments. Those attempts require making unverifiable assumptions about the individuals who own corporations and thus pay the corporate taxes.

Why does this matter? Because critics of our flat tax often misleadingly compare the flat tax to a windfall for the rich. Other critics compare the tax on wages in the flat-tax plan with the tax reported on Form 1040, which includes a variety of nonwage income and a raft of special deductions. A proper comparison must include all types of income—business income, interest, dividends, wages, and so forth—and assign total income to individuals in income categories to see how those categories of individuals fare under Hall-Rabushka versus under current law. This is not an easy exercise for academics or politicians. It sounds complicated, but it is a crucial aspect of the debate on fairness and fair shares. We will return to this point after we set forth the details of our plan. For now we just want to emphasize that any fair comparison of two alternative tax systems by income category must include corporate income taxes as well as individual taxes.

Consumption Taxes

An increasing number of economists and politicians are proposing that federal income taxes be reconstituted as consumption taxes. As the name suggests, a consumption tax is a tax on spending rather than income. Consumption taxes are growing in popularity because, by exempting investment or savings from taxation, they would encourage saving and stimulate capital formation. Put another way, the underlying concept of consumption taxes is that individuals would be taxed on what they take out of the economy (when they spend money to consume), not on what they produce (reflected in working and saving).

Consumption taxes take many forms. In one form, a family would pay a *cash-flow expenditure tax* on the basis of its total income minus saving. The forms for computing individual income tax would contain lines to report deposits into various forms of savings instruments (a deduction) and money withdrawn from savings instruments or borrowed funds used for spending (an addition). The consumer would pay the tax directly.

Another form of consumption tax is the *value-added tax*, or VAT, which is levied on goods and services at each stage of production through the retail level; it is collected from the seller. Some percentage rate is levied on the difference between a firm's sales and its purchases, and this sum is incorporated into the price of the object (and, commensurately, the consumer price level). It is widely used in Europe.

Yet another form is the *sales tax*, which is levied on the sales of goods and services and is also collected from the consumer by the seller. Sales taxes are in use in virtually every state in the union and are regarded as the preserve of state and local governments in the United States.

The plan we set forth in chapter 3 is a tax on consumption that differs from the cash-flow expenditure tax, the European-style VAT, or a national sales tax. Rather, it is a comprehensive income tax (the base is GDP) with a 100 percent immediate write-off of all business investment at the level of the business enterprise. It is a consumption tax because it removes all investment spending from the tax base.

The justification for consumption taxes rests on their built-in incentives to save and invest. By exempting investment from taxation, consumption taxes encourage investment and discourage spending. (Over time, each act of investment traces back to an act of saving; thus exempting investment from the tax base amounts to exempting saving.) Chapter 4 presents some estimates of the impact that a full-fledged, flat-rate consumption tax would have on growth.

TAX RATES, TAX BURDENS, AND FAIR SHARES

After explaining our flat-tax proposal in chapter 3, in chapter 4 we subject it to every reasonable test of fairness and examine how different categories of taxpayers would fare as against the current code. But there exists a body of evidence from U.S. tax history that is pertinent to this chapter's discussion of taxes and fairness. Three episodes of major changes in tax legislation in the 1920s, 1960s, and 1980s suggest that cutting tax rates causes the rich to pay a higher share of the tax burden. In other words, the most effective way to increase progressivity and collect more taxes from the rich is to lower, not raise, marginal rates of taxation.

Table 2.1   Effects of Mellon Tax Cuts

| | Tax Revenues Collected (in millions of 1929 constant dollars) | | | Percentage of Tax Revenues Collected from Each Group | |
Income Category	1921	1926	Percent Change	1921	1926
Less than $10,000	$155	$33	−79%	21%	5%
$10,000 to $25,000	122	70	−43	18	10
$25,000 to $50,000	108	109	+1	16	15
$50,000 to $100,000	111	137	+23	16	19
Over $100,000	194	362	+86	29	51

Andrew Mellon and the 1920s

Recall that the first income tax of 1913 imposed rates that ranged from 1 to 7 percent; wartime needs for revenue increased the tax rate structure almost overnight, to a range of 6 to 77 percent. When peace returned, the wartime structure of tax rates came under the ax of Secretary of the Treasury Andrew Mellon, who cut the top rate to 25 percent.

Professors James Gwartney and Richard Stroup have analyzed tax receipts by income categories before and after the Mellon reductions. After the reductions, the highest income category paid substantially more in absolute tax dollars and nearly doubled its share of total federal revenues. The lowest income category paid almost 80 percent less in absolute dollars, and its share of the total burden fell from 23 to 5 percent (see table 2.1).

To repeat, cutting the top rate from 77 percent to 25 percent produced a more progressive tax system.

How can this be? How can a massive windfall to the rich cause them to pay more in federal income taxes? Why do lower rates increase progressivity? One big reason is that formerly high-bracket taxpayers shifted assets from tax-free bonds into productive outlets. Even though the rate reductions were greatest for higher-income brackets, the 1920s cuts shifted the tax burden to that area. The tax base proved highly responsive to changes in the incentive structure during the Mellon years.

This is not a book about the pros and cons of tax-free municipal bonds or hundreds of other specific loopholes. There are plenty of highly paid professional lobbyists in Washington, D.C., who will defend each specific loophole, no matter how bizarre. The important point here is that high rates shrink the tax base by encouraging individuals to seek tax-free income. Low rates increase the tax base by rewarding individuals who earn higher taxable incomes. A broad-based, low-rate tax system is the best route to progressivity.

John F. Kennedy and the 1960s

Republican appointee Andrew Mellon's 1920s rate cut was not a unique episode in U.S. tax history. President John F. Kennedy, a Democrat, took up the same cudgel to cut marginal tax rates across the board in his term of office. Proposed in 1963 and signed into law in March 1964, Kennedy's legislation reduced all brackets, from a

Table 2.2   The Effects of 1964 Tax Cuts on
Upper-Income Taxpayers

	Taxpayers Earning $50,000– $100,000	*Taxpayers Earning $100,000– $500,000*	*Taxpayers Earning over $500,000*
Tax paid, old law	$3.622 billion	$2.405 billion	$701 million
Tax paid, new law	$3.693 billion	$2.780 billion	$1.020 billion

range of 20 to 91 percent to 14 to 70 percent. In dollar terms, about 70 percent of the estimated total reduction of $5.5 billion would go to taxpayers making less than $10,000, who made up 84 percent of all taxpayers and who bore 48 percent of the income tax burden. Although the largest *dollar amount* went to taxpayers of modest means, the largest *percentage cut* applied to those with taxable incomes over $500,000.

Using income data reported by the IRS, Lawrence B. Lindsey compared taxes paid by high-income taxpayers before and after the 1964 rate reductions. In 1965, the first year for which the new rates applied, high-income taxpayers declared more taxable income and paid more in taxes than they would have paid under the old law. The trend was especially pronounced in the highest bracket (see table 2.2).

Lindsey offers three reasons why lower rates increased the share of taxes paid by the rich. One, taxpayers in the highest brackets shifted money from consumption or tax-sheltered investments into more productive, taxable investments; tax avoidance declined. Two, taxpayers became more honest as evasion became less rewarding; tax evasion declined. Three, some taxpayers, rewarded by higher after-tax returns, worked harder; incentives improved.

Ronald Reagan and the 1980s

The 1980s provide the best evidence that lower tax rates increase the fairness of the tax system. Between 1981 and 1986, marginal tax rates were reduced across the board, although the full rate reduction in the 1981 Economic Recovery Tax Act did not take effect until January 1, 1984. The Tax Reform Act of 1986 further reduced the top rate of 50 percent to 28 percent. How did the rich respond? The share of total individual income taxes paid by the top 1 percent (by adjusted gross income category) rose from 17.9 percent in 1981 to 25.6 percent in 1990 (see table 2.3). The share paid by the top 5 percent rose from 35.4 percent to 44 percent and by the top 10 percent from 48.2 percent to 55.7 percent. The bottom 50 percent reduced its contribution from 7.4 percent in 1981 to 5.7 percent in 1990.

Why did the cuts in marginal rates increase the tax burden on the rich? As before, when tax rates fall, upper-income households shift assets out of instruments that generate tax-exempt income, or from schemes that are designed to shelter income, into taxable economic activity. In 1986, federal tax expenditures, items that represent revenue lost from loopholes, amounted to $500

Table 2.3   Share of Total Federal Individual Income
Tax Burdenby Adjusted Gross Income Percentile

Tax Year	Top 1 Percentile	Top 5 Percentile	Top 10 Percentile	Top 25 Percentile	Top 50 Percentile
1980	19.3%	37.9%	49.5%	73.1%	92.9%
1981	17.9	35.4	48.2	72.4	92.6
1982	19.3	35.4	48.8	72.6	92.7
1983	20.7	37.7	50.1	73.3	92.9
1984	21.8	38.6	51.1	73.8	92.7
1985	22.3	39.3	51.9	74.3	92.9
1986	25.8	42.7	54.9	76.0	93.5
1987	24.8	43.3	55.5	76.9	93.9
1988	27.6	45.8	57.3	77.8	94.3
1989	25.2	43.9	55.8	77.2	94.2
1990	25.6	44.0	55.7	77.2	94.3
1991	24.7	43.5	55.4	77.3	94.5

Source: Internal Revenue Service, Statistics of Income Division, unpublished data.

billion. By 1990, the figure had fallen to $400 billion. More than $100 billion of activity was brought into the tax net, largely by individuals in the former high brackets. Lower rates also curbed tax evasion.

The 1990 budget accord raised the top personal tax rate from 28 percent to 31 percent. This marginal tax rate increase was part of President George Bush's $500 billion deficit reduction package, negotiated with the leadership of Congress. For married filing jointly, the 31 percent rate applied to taxable income over $82,150 (equivalent to adjusted gross income over $100,000);

this bracket constitutes the top 3.3 percent of the income distribution.

The IRS statistics for 1991, the first taxable year following the 1990 tax rate increase, reveal that the super-rich, the top 1 percent of income distribution, and the ordinary rich, the top 5 percent, both paid smaller shares of total income taxes in 1991 than in 1990. The new, higher tax rate in the 1990 law reduced the progressivity of the system, making it less fair. We expect that IRS statistics for 1994 and beyond will show that less fairness, not more, was the most visible consequence of the 1993 tax increase legislation. Political rhetoric is no match for evidence when it comes to real tax fairness.

Tax Rates and Economic Behavior

Although it seems obvious that tax rate increases affect economic behavior, this point is denied by the fair-share proponents of higher tax rates on the rich and is not fully incorporated in the economic models of the Treasury, the Joint Committee on Taxation, or the Congressional Budget Office, which accounts for the "static" revenue gains and losses when they calculate the revenue impact of changes in tax rates. To dispute that higher tax rates discourage economic activity is to repudiate the one genuine law in economics—the law of demand—which stipulates that prices and quantities are inversely related. Consumers understand the effect of changes in price. When prices fall, they buy more of an item; when prices rise, they buy less.

Higher tax rates discourage economic activity.
Higher tax rates reduce the demand to work, save,
and invest by reducing after-tax rates of return. Lower
tax rates increase the demand to work, save, and invest
by increasing after-tax rates of return. Evidence for the
adverse effect of higher tax rates is seen by compar-
ing the government's projections of new revenues attached to tax increase legislation with the actual revenues.

For example, consider the Tax Reform Act of 1986,
which raised the maximum capital gains tax rate from
20 percent to 28 percent. (In chapter 3 we discuss the
right way to tax capital gains.) Capital gains realizations
fell sharply, from $350 billion in 1986 to an annual
range of $100—150 billion during 1987—1991. Treas-
ury and Congressional Budget Office (CBO) predictions
of capital gains realizations for 1987—1991 were far
higher, by several hundred billion dollars, than actual
reported gains. In January 1990, for example, the CBO
projected that capital gains in 1991 would total $269
billion; the actual figure turned out to be only $108
billion. As a result, revenues from capital gains fell
sharply. The loss in anticipated capital gains revenues
amounted to about half a percent of GDP. The fall in
realized gains was more dramatic among the middle
three-fifths of taxpayers than among the top 20 percent
because taxpayers with incomes as low as $22,100 saw
their effective capital gains tax rate increase from 14
percent to 28 percent, while those taxpayers in the top
bracket experienced a somewhat smaller fractional rise,
from 20 percent to 28 percent. Half a percent of GDP

in anticipated capital gains taxes that failed to materialize amounts to about $30 billion. The reason for the gross overestimate of capital gains realizations is that the CBO did not take into account the fact that taxpayers, facing sharply higher taxes on capital gains, significantly reduced their sales of assets at all income levels.

So why do supporters of higher tax rates cling to a price-free model of human behavior? They point to something known as the target income hypothesis, which posits that people work and invest to attain a target level of after-tax income. In this view, higher tax rates will encourage people to work harder and save more. If this proposition were remotely true, the country should consider returning to the 91 percent top marginal tax rate of the 1950s to get the most effort and savings from the most productive segment of the population. A hidden implication in this argument is that the government should impose higher tax rates on poverty-level and lower-middle-income households, which will force them to work harder to keep from slipping further into poverty.

In the midst of mythology, Congress discovered one verity—the price effect of taxes matters. As previously described, both houses of Congress agreed to repeal the 10 percent luxury tax on boats, jewelry, furs, and airplanes that wreaked havoc in those sectors. The reason is that this tax, by raising prices, reduced demand, lowered sales, put people out of work, and lost revenues.

BIPARTISAN SUPPORT FOR THE FLAT TAX

Almost from its modern inception, the flat tax enjoyed bipartisan support. Our involvement began with an article we wrote for the *Wall Street Journal* on December 10, 1981, in which we first proposed our flat-rate tax. The public, media, and politicians latched onto the flat tax as a vehicle for radically simplifying and reforming the federal income tax, making it a widely discussed issue for more than a decade. Members of Congress have introduced numerous flat-tax proposals since 1982; our proposal has been introduced in almost every Congress since then.

The flat tax was not a partisan idea in origin or spirit. Senator Dennis DeConcini of Arizona, a Democrat, introduced one of the first bills (S. 2147) on March 1, 1982, after extensive consultation with us—his bill, in effect, was our plan. Representative Leon Panetta of California, also a Democrat, introduced a similar bill on April 5, 1982. Republicans too, including Representative Phil Crane of Illinois, introduced a different form of the flat tax.

Senator Steve Symms of Idaho, a Republican, joined Senator DeConcini in reintroducing the Hall-Rabushka flat tax in 1983 and again in 1985. In 1983, members of both parties rushed in alternative plans; the most publicized were those of Democrats Bill Bradley and Richard Gephardt and Republicans Bob Kasten and Jack Kemp.

Why did the flat tax enjoy bipartisan support? Liberals strongly believe in a progressive tax system, which for them means that rich people should pay a higher share of their income in taxes than other people, and have relied on the graduated rate structure to achieve this goal. Congress, however, has inserted hundreds of loopholes into the tax code that allowed some very rich people to pay little or nothing in taxes. Liberal supporters of the flat tax, correctly observing that the progressive rates in the tax code were steeply at odds with reality, also feared that evasion and avoidance could reduce the flow of revenues to Washington, D.C., jeopardizing spending programs they considered valuable.

On the right, conservatives, who believe strongly in a free market economy, argue that high marginal tax rates harm incentives to work, save, and invest. High rates, they say, penalize success, discourage risk taking, and impose a levy on some forms of income at confiscatory levels. A flat rate avoids penalizing success, ends bracket creep once and for all, removes the penalty on marriage, and taxes all returns to effort and savings at the same low rate.

In the middle, millions of taxpayers in the American mainstream, exasperated by the unfathomable complexity and high costs of compliance and offended by an upsurge in tax cheating, find the flat tax to be an attractive alternative. They especially like the idea that a tax return could fit on a postcard, taking a few minutes to complete, with everyone bound by the same rules.

In universities and think tanks, the dozens of scholars who have studied the flat tax generally agree that the current graduated-rate tax code distorts the flow of resources in the economy, with losses to economic welfare in the hundreds of billions of dollars. They acknowledge that adopting a flat tax would improve economic efficiency and, over time, generate higher revenues than the current system. Indeed, the preamble to several flat-tax proposals offered by moderate Democrats in the 1980s began with the premise that high tax rates damage investment and weaken the performance of our economy.

The Tax Reform Act of 1986, which reduced the top rate to 28 percent, took the steam out of the flat-tax movement, for it completed a process of rate reductions in the 1980s that brought the top rate down from 70 percent to 28 percent, certainly closer to our 19 percent rate. The 1986 act also truncated the tax code from more than a dozen brackets in 1980 to just two brackets, 15 and 28 percent. Two brackets with a relatively low top rate came close to accomplishing one goal of tax reform: eliminating the disincentive costs of high rates. However, it left unresolved the issues of complexity and high compliance costs.

Reviving the Flat Tax

The flat tax sprang back to life from an unlikely source, former California Governor Jerry Brown. As a candidate for the Democratic Party's presidential nomination in 1992, Brown endorsed the flat tax for three reasons: (1) to eliminate the power of special interests to buy favors from the tax-writing committees of Congress by closing almost every loophole; (2) to simplify the system so that everyone could understand their tax obligations and easily file their returns; and (3) to improve economic performance by dramatically slashing tax rates. These reasons blend fairness with efficiency. Few would contend that Jerry Brown wanted to give a tax break to the rich.

At the same time, Republican Bruce Herschensohn, candidate for the U.S. Senate from California, made the flat tax a centerpiece of his campaign. Herschensohn, on the far right of the political spectrum, ran on the flat tax for three reasons: (1) to improve incentives and increase growth; (2) to simplify the tax code; and (3) to reduce the costs of compliance. Brown and Herschensohn, had they been victorious, would have made an odd couple.

Brown and Herschensohn differed on the specifics. Brown proposed a version developed by Arthur Laffer, a combination personal income tax and cash-flow expenditure business tax, both assessed at a 13 percent rate, which also incorporated Social Security taxes. Herschensohn ran on our plan. As a presidential candidate who in late March 1992 was Clinton's principal remaining opponent, Brown's version of the flat tax came under intense media scrutiny.

The Media and the Flat Tax

The dominant media were not kind to Brown. The *New York Times* editorial page said, "Tilted"; *Business Week* said, "'Jerry's Tax': Wrong Answer, Right Questions"; *U.S. News & World Report* labeled it "Brown's new fad," saying, "It's not by any means as simple—or quite as fair—as it sounds"; and *Fortune* said it was "half-baked."

But these same commentators gave Hall-Rabushka rave reviews. Perhaps the strongest endorsement was printed as the lead editorial in the March 27, 1992, edition of the *New York Times*.

> Taking Jerry Brown seriously means taking his flat tax proposal seriously. Needlessly, he's made that hard to do. By being careless, the former California Governor has bent a good idea out of shape. He could fix it, but until he does, Bill Clinton is right to attack the plan as a budget-buster and a dagger aimed at poor families.
>
> Mr. Brown's basic idea—creating a simplified code that encourages saving—is exactly right. But he ignores all-important details. The tragedy is that his cavalier attitude has armed his critics to denounce the one truly creative and important idea to emerge from the Presidential campaign.
>
> The present tax code is riddled with wasteful contradictions and complexity. For example, profit from corporate investment is taxed twice—when earned by the corporation and again when distributed to shareholders. That powerfully discourages savings and investment—the exact opposite of what the economy needs to grow.
>
> The remedy is, in a word, integration, meshing personal and corporate codes so that the brunt of taxes fall on consumption, not saving. Tax reform should also simplify the code, making loopholes harder for Congress to disguise, and enact. And for reasons of elemental decency, tax reform shouldn't come at the expense of the poor.
>
> *Remarkably, there is a reform that achieves all*

these objectives. Robert Hall and Alvin Rabushka, economists at the Hoover Institution, have proposed an integrated code that applies a single rate to both personal and corporate income [italics added].

The editorial went on to explain how Hall-Rabushka, in contrast to Brown, accomplished complete integration, simplification, progressivity, and revenue neutrality.

The day before, the *Wall Street Journal* acknowledged that it was "favorably inclined toward the flat tax. Economists Robert Hall and Alvin Rabushka of Stanford have popularized the concept on this page."

On May 4, 1992, *Fortune* stated that "Flat is Beautiful."

A well-designed flatter tax system would merely tax all income at a single low rate and could easily be made progressive. The one designed by Hoover Institution economists Robert E. Hall and Alvin Rabushka, for instance, would tax individual and corporate income at 19% — not coincidentally, about the total burden of the median family income. But it would pass over the poor and maintain progressivity by including generous personal exemptions.

What would make those lower rates sit up and work, of course, is that virtually all loopholes and deductions would disappear. The economic benefits are twofold and powerful: The flat tax would take nearly all the complexity out of the code, and it would put an end to most unproductive taxophobic behavior. Those were the goals of the tax reform movement of the early 1980s, and were partly achieved in 1986. Why not finish the job?

Peter Passell wrote in the *New York Times* of April 1, 1992, that Brown's consumption tax, a European-style VAT, or new gasoline taxes were inferior alternatives to "the clever direct consumption taxes devised in the mid-1980s by Robert Hall and Alvin Rabushka of the Hoover Institution at Stanford University." *Forbes* called the previous edition of our book, *The Flat Tax*, the bible of the flat-tax movement.

3. The Postcard Tax Return

TAX FORMS really can fit on postcards. A cleanly designed tax system takes only a few elementary calculations, in contrast to the hopeless complexity of today's income taxes. In this chapter, we present a complete plan for a whole new tax system that puts a low tax rate on a comprehensive definition of income. Because its base is broad, the astonishingly low 19 percent tax rate raises the same revenue as does the current tax system. The tax on families is fair and progressive: the poor pay no tax at all, and the fraction of income that a family pays rises with income. The system is simple and easy to understand. And the tax operates on the consumption tax principle—families are taxed on what they take out of the economy, not what they put into it.

Our system rests on a basic administrative principle: income should be taxed exactly once as close as possible to its source. Today's tax system violates this principle in all sorts of ways. Some kinds of income—like fringe benefits—are never taxed at all. Other kinds, like dividends and capital gains, are taxed twice. And interest income, which is supposed to be taxed once, escapes taxation completely in all too many cases where clever taxpayers arrange to receive interest beyond the reach of the IRS.

Under our plan, all income is taxed at the same rate. Equality of tax rates is a basic concept of the flat tax. Its logic is much more profound than just the simplicity of calculation with a single tax rate. Whenever different forms of income are taxed at different rates or different taxpayers face different rates, the public figures out how to take advantage of the differential. The basic trick is to take deductions at the highest available rate and to report income at the lowest rate. Here are some of the ways that the trick can be applied:

- A company pays its workers partly in the form of stock options because the options will eventually be taxed at lower capital gains rates.

- A real estate operator borrows from a bank and deducts the interest at his 40 percent marginal rate; the interest received by the depositors at the bank is taxed at their lower rates.

- An author arranges for royalties to be deferred to next year because she knows that she will be in a lower tax bracket next year.

- A corporation pays its shareholders exaggerated salaries as officers because salaries are taxed only once but dividends are taxed twice.

- A company gives its workers prepaid legal services as a nontaxable fringe benefit, in place of cash that would be taxed.

Our plan would sweep away all these inequities and inefficiencies. None of these opportunities to escape taxes by distorting economic choices would survive our reform.

PROGRESSIVITY, EFFICIENCY, AND SIMPLICITY

Limiting the burden of taxes on the poor is a central principle of tax reform. Some ideas for tax simplification and reform flout this principle—neither a federal sales tax nor a value-added tax is progressive. Instead, all citizens, rich and poor alike, pay essentially the same fraction of their spending in taxes. We reject sales and value-added taxes for this reason. The current federal tax system avoids taxing the poor, and we think it should stay that way.

Exempting the poor from taxes does not require graduated tax rates rising to high levels for upper-income families. A flat rate, applied to all income above a generous personal allowance, provides progressivity without creating important differences in tax rates. Graduated taxes automatically create differences in tax rates among taxpayers, with all the attendant opportunities for tax avoidance tricks. Because it is high-income taxpayers who have the biggest incentive and the best opportunity to use special tricks to exploit tax rate differentials, applying the same tax rate to these taxpayers for all their income in all years is the most important goal of flat-rate taxation.

Our proposal is based squarely on the principle of consumption taxation. Saving is untaxed, thus solving the problem that has perplexed the designers of the current tax system, which contains an incredible hodge-podge of savings and investment incentives. As a general matter, the current system puts substantial taxes on the earnings from savings. On that account, the economy is biased toward too little saving and too much consumption. But Congress has inserted a number of special provisions to spur saving. Most important, saving for retirement is excused from current taxation. Workers are not taxed on the amount their employers contribute to pension funds, and the employers can deduct those contributions. The self-employed can take advantage of the same opportunity with Keogh, individual retirement account (IRA), and simplified employee pension (SEP) plans. The overall effect of the existing incentives is spotty—there are excessive incentives for some saving-investment channels and inadequate incentives for others. In our system, there is a single, coherent provision for taxing the return to saving. All income is taxed, but the earnings from saved income are not taxed further. We will explain how this works later in the chapter.

We believe that the simplicity of our system is a central feature. Complex tax forms and tax laws do more harm than just deforesting America. Complicated taxes require expensive advisers for taxpayers and equally expensive reviews and audits by the government. A complex tax invites the taxpayer to search for special features to exploit to the disadvantage of the rest of us. And complex taxes diminish confidence in government, inviting a breakdown in cooperation with the tax system and the spread of outright evasion.

AN INTEGRATED FLAT TAX

Our flat tax applies to both businesses and individuals. Although our system has two separate tax forms—one

for business income and the other for wages and salaries—it is an integrated system. When we speak of its
virtues, such as its equal taxation of all types of income,
we mean the system, not one of its two parts. As we will
explain, the business tax is not just a replacement for
the existing corporate income tax. It covers all businesses, not just corporations. And it covers interest income, which is currently taxed under the personal income tax.

In our system, all income is classified as either business income or wages (including salaries and retirement
benefits). The system is airtight. Taxes on both types of
income are equal. The wage tax has features to make
the overall system progressive. Both taxes have postcard
forms. The low tax rate of 19 percent is enough to
match the revenue of the federal tax system as it existed
in 1993, the last full year of data available as we write.

Here is the logic of our system, stripped to basics:
We want to tax consumption. The public does one of
two things with its income—spends it or invests it. We
can measure consumption as income minus investment.
A really simple tax would just have each firm pay tax
on the total amount of income generated by the firm
less that firm's investment in plant and equipment. The
value-added tax works just that way. But a value-added
tax is unfair because it is not progressive. That's why we
break the tax in two. The firm pays tax on all the income
generated at the firm except the income paid to its workers. The workers pay tax on what they earn, and the tax
they pay is progressive.

To measure the total amount of income generated

at a business, the best approach is to take the total receipts of the firm over the year and subtract the payments the firm has made to its workers and suppliers. This approach guarantees a comprehensive tax base. The successful value-added taxes in Europe work this way. The base for the business tax is the following:

Total revenue from sales of goods and services

less

purchases of inputs from other firms

less

wages, salaries, and pensions paid to workers

less

purchases of plant and equipment

The other piece is the wage tax. Each family pays 19 percent of its wage, salary, and pension income over a family allowance (the allowance makes the system progressive). The base for the compensation tax is total wages, salaries, and retirement benefits less the total amount of family allowances.

Table 3.1 is a calculation of flat-tax revenue based on the U.S. National Income and Product Accounts for 1993. The first line shows gross domestic product, the most comprehensive measure of income throughout the economy. The next line is indirect business taxes that are included in GDP but that would not be taxed under the flat tax, such as sales and excise taxes. Line 3, income included in GDP but not in the tax base, is mostly the value of houses owned and lived in by families; this income does not go through the market. Wages, salaries, and pensions, line 4, would be reported on the first line

Table 3.1   Flat-Tax Revenues Compared with
Current Revenues

Line	Income or Revenue	Billions of Dollars
1	Gross domestic product	$6,374
2	Indirect business tax	431
3	Income included in GDP but not in tax base	217
4	Wages, salaries, and pensions	3,100
5	Investment	723
6	Business-tax base (line 1 minus lines 2 through 5)	1,903
7	Business-tax revenue (19 percent of line 6)	362
8	Family allowances	1,705
9	Wage-tax base (line 4 less line 8)	1,395
10	Wage-tax revenue (19 percent of line 9)	265
11	Total flat-tax revenue (line 7 plus line 10)	627
12	Actual personal income tax	510
13	Actual corporate income tax	118
14	Total actual revenue (line 12 plus line 13)	627

of the wage-tax form and would be deducted by businesses. Investment, line 5, is the amount spent by businesses purchasing new plant and equipment (each business could also deduct its purchases of used plant and equipment, but these would be included in the taxable income of the selling business and would net out in the aggregate). Line 6 shows the taxable income of all businesses after they have deducted their wages and investment. The revenue from the business tax, line 7, is 19 percent of the tax base on line 6. Line 8 shows the amount of family allowances that would be deducted.

The wage-tax base on line 9 shows the amount of wages, salaries, and pensions left after deducting all family allowances from the amount on line 4. The wage-tax revenue on line 10 is 19 percent of the base. Total flat-tax revenue on line 11 is $627 billion. Lines 12 and 13 show the actual revenue from the personal and corporate income taxes. The total actual revenue on line 14 is also $627 billion. The flat-tax revenue and the actual revenue are the same, by design. We propose to reproduce the revenue of the actual income tax system, not to raise or lower it.

These computations show that in 1993 the revenue from the corporate income tax, with a tax rate of 35 percent, was $118 billion. The revenue from our business tax at a rate of 19 percent would have been $362 billion, just over three times as much, even though the tax rate is not much more than half the current corporate rate. There are three main reasons that the flat business tax yields more revenue than does the existing corporate tax. First, slightly more than half of business income is from noncorporate businesses—professional partnerships, proprietorships, and the like. Second, our business tax does not permit the deduction of interest paid by businesses, whereas the corporate income tax does. Third, the business tax puts a tax on fringe benefits, which escape any taxation in the current system.

The substantial revenue the government would derive from the flat business tax is the key to the fairness of our tax system. Because most business income goes to the rich, putting an airtight tax of 19 percent on that income permits taxes and tax rates on working people to be lowered.

The other side of the coin, of course, is that our wage tax would yield less revenue than does the current personal income tax—$265 billion in 1993 as against $510 billion. We are not proposing a massive shift in taxes from wages to capital income. Our wage tax applies just to wages, salaries, and private pensions, whereas today's personal income tax includes unincorporated business income, dividends, interest, rent, and many other kinds of income that we tax as part of business income. The switch to the more reliable principle of taxing business income at the source, rather than hoping to catch the income at the destination, is one reason that the business tax yields so much more revenue than does the corporate tax.

Our calculations assume that the IRS will learn about all the income currently counted in the national income accounts except the $217 billion allowed for in line 3 of table 3.1. The national income accounts are based primarily on income tax data but do make some projections for unreported income. On the one hand, it is possible that our estimates of the base for the flat tax are a little optimistic. On the other hand, our calculations of the amount of family allowances at line 8 definitely overstate the total dollar amount of the allowances. Another limitation on our calculations is that we do not consider the way the economy would respond to tax reform. In chapter 4, we discuss why the flat tax would increase national income and tax revenue. But part of that process might involve a burst of investment, which would temporarily depress flat-tax revenue because of the expensing of investment. Only a detailed analysis using data not available to us would determine whether we have over- or underestimated the revenue from the flat tax. We do not think we are far off, however.

The Individual Wage Tax

The individual wage tax has a single purpose—to tax the large fraction of income that employers pay as cash to their workers. It is not a tax system by itself but is one of the two major parts of the complete system. The base of the tax is defined narrowly and precisely as actual payments of wages, salaries, and pensions. Pension contributions and other fringe benefits paid by employers are not counted as part of wages. In other words, the tax on pension income is paid when the retired worker actually receives the pension, not when the employer sets aside the money to pay the future pension. This principle applies even if the employer pays into a completely separate pension fund, if the worker makes a voluntary contribution to a 401(k) program, or if the worker contributes to a Keogh, IRA, or SEP fund.

The tax form for our wage tax is self-explanatory (see figure 3.1). To make the tax system progressive, only earnings over a personal or family allowance are taxed. The allowance is $25,500 for a family of four in 1995 but would rise with the cost of living in later years. All the taxpayer has to do is report total wages, salaries, and pensions at the top, compute the family allowance based

Form 1	Individual Wage Tax		1998
Your first name and initial (if joint return, also give spouse's name and initial)		Last name	Your social security number
Present home address (number and street including apartment number or rural route)			Spouse's social security number
City, town, or post office, state, and ZIP code		Your occupation™	
		Spouse's occupation™	

1	Wages and salary.........	1
2	Pension and retirement benefits.........	2
3	Total compensation (line 1 plus line 2).........	3
4	Personal allowance	
	(a) ☐ $16,500 for married filing jointly.........	4(a)
	(b) ☐ $9,500 for single.........	4(b)
	(c) ☐ $14,000 for single head of household.........	4(c)
5	Number of dependents, not including spouse.........	5
6	Personal allowances for dependents (line 5 multiplied by $4,500).........	6
7	Total personal allowances (line 4 plus line 6).........	7
8	Taxable compensation (line 3 less line 7, if positive; otherwise zero).........	8
9	Tax (19% of line 8).........	9
10	Tax withheld by employer.........	10
11	Tax due (line 9 less line 10, if positive).........	11
12	Refund due (line 10 less line 9, if positive).........	12

Figure 3.1   Individual Wage-Tax Form

on marital status and number of dependents, subtract
the allowance, multiply by 19 percent to compute the
tax, take account of withholding, and pay the difference
or apply for a refund. For about 80 percent of the population, filling out this postcard once a year would be
the only effort needed to satisfy the Internal Revenue
Service. What a change from the many pages of schedules the frustrated taxpayer fills out today!

For the 80 percent of taxpayers who don't run businesses, the individual wage tax would be the only tax to
worry about. Many features of current taxes would disappear, including charitable deductions, mortgage interest deductions, capital gains taxes, dividend taxes, and
interest taxes. (We discuss these in detail later.)

Anyone who is self-employed or pays expenses directly in connection with making a living will need to
file the business tax to get the proper deduction for expenses. Fortunately, the business-tax form is even simpler than the wage-tax form.

Again, we stress that the wage tax is not a complete
income tax on individuals; it taxes only wages, salaries,
and pensions. The companion business tax picks up all
other components of income. Together they form an
airtight tax system.

The Business Tax

It is not the purpose of the business tax to tax businesses.
Fundamentally, people pay taxes, not businesses. The
idea of the business tax is to collect the tax that the
owners of a business owe on the income produced by

the business. Collecting business income tax at the source of the income avoids one of the biggest causes of leakage in the tax system today: Interest can pass through many layers where it is invariably deducted when it is paid out but frequently not reported as income.

Airtight taxation of individual business income at the source is possible because we already know the tax rate of all of the owners of the business—it is the common flat rate paid by all taxpayers. If the tax system has graduated rates, taxation at the source becomes a problem. If each owner is to be taxed at that owner's rate, the business would have to find out the tax rate applicable to each owner and apply that rate to the income produced in the business for that owner. But this is only the beginning of the problem. The IRS would have to audit a business and its owners together to see that the owners were reporting the correct tax rates to the business. Further, suppose one of the owners made a mistake and was later discovered to be in a higher tax bracket. Then the business would have to refile its tax form to collect the right tax. Obviously this wouldn't work. Business taxes have to be collected at the destination, from the owners, if graduated rates are to be applied. Source taxation is only practical when a single rate is applied to all owners. Because source taxation is reliable and inexpensive, it is a powerful practical argument for using a single rate for all business income.

The business tax is a giant, comprehensive withholding tax on all types of income other than wages, salaries, and pensions. It is carefully designed to tax every bit of income outside of wages but to tax it only once. The business tax does not have deductions for interest payments, dividends, or any other type of payment to the owners of the business. As a result, all income that people receive from business activity has already been taxed. Because the tax has already been paid, the tax system does not need to worry about what happens to interest, dividends, or capital gains after these types of income leave the firm, resulting in an enormously simplified and improved tax system. Today, the IRS receives more than a billion Form 1099s, which keep track of interest and dividends, and must make an overwhelming effort to match these forms to the 1040s filed by the recipients. The only reason for a Form 1099 is to track income as it makes its way from the business where it originates to the ultimate recipient. Not a single Form 1099 would be needed under a flat tax with business income taxed at the source.

The way that we have set up the business tax is not arbitrary—on the contrary, it is dictated by the principles we set forth at the beginning of this chapter. The tax would be assessed on all the income originating in a business but not on any income that originates in other businesses or on the wages, salaries, and pensions paid to employees. The types of income taxed by the business tax would include

- Profits from the use of plant and equipment

- Profits from ideas embodied in copyrights, patents, trade secrets, and the like

- Profits from past organization-building, marketing, and advertising efforts

- Earnings of key executives and others who are owners as well as employees and who are paid less than they contribute to the business

- Earnings of doctors, lawyers, and other professionals who have businesses organized as proprietorships or partnerships

- Rent earned from apartments and other real estate

- Fringe benefits provided to workers

All a business's income derives from the sale of its products and services. On the top line of the business-tax form (see figure 3.2) goes the gross sales of the business—its proceeds from the sale of all its products. But some of the proceeds come from the resale of inputs and parts the firm purchased; the tax has already been paid on those items because the seller also has to pay the business tax. Thus, the firm can deduct the cost of all the goods, materials, and services it purchases to make the product it sells. In addition, it can deduct its wages, salaries, and pensions, for, under our wage tax, the taxes on those will be paid by the workers receiving them. Finally, the business can deduct all its outlays for plant, equipment, and land. (Later we will explain why this investment incentive is the right one.)

Everything left from this calculation is the income originating in the firm and is taxed at the flat rate of 19 percent. In most businesses, there is enough left that the prospective revenue from the business tax is the $362

Form 2	Business Tax		1998
Business name			Employer identification number
Street address			County
City, state, and ZIP code			Principal product
1	Gross revenue from sales.	1	
2	Allowable costs		
	(a) Purchases of goods, services, and materials.	2(a)	
	(b) Wages, salaries, and pensions.	2(b)	
	(c) Purchases of capital equipment, structures, and land.	2(c)	
3	Total allowable costs (sum of lines 2(a), 2(b), 2(c)).	3	
4	Taxable income (line 1 less line 3).	4	
5	Tax (19% of line 4).	5	
6	Carry-forward from 1997.	6	
7	Interest on carry-forward (6% of line 6).	7	
8	Carry-forward into 1998 (line 6 plus line 7).	8	
9	Tax due (line 5 less line 8, if positive).	9	
10	Carry-forward to 1999 (line 8 less line 5, if positive).	10	

Figure 3.2   Business-Tax Form

billion we computed earlier. Many deductions allowed to businesses under current laws are eliminated in our plan, including interest payments and fringe benefits. But our excluding these deductions is not an arbitrary move to increase the tax base. In all cases, eliminating deductions, when combined with the other features of our system, moves toward the goal of taxing all income once at a common, low rate and achieving a broad consumption tax.

Eliminating the deduction for interest paid by businesses is a central part of our general plan to tax business income at the source. It makes sense because we propose not to tax interest received by individuals. The tax that the government now hopes (sometimes in vain) that individuals will pay will assuredly be paid by the business itself.

We sweep away the whole complicated apparatus of depreciation deductions, but we replace it with something more favorable for capital formation, an immediate 100 percent first-year tax write-off of all investment spending. Sometimes this approach is called expensing of investment; it is standard in the value-added approach to consumption taxation. In other words, we don't deny depreciation deductions; we enhance them. More on this shortly.

Fringe benefits are outside the current tax system entirely, which makes no sense. The cost of fringes is deductible by businesses, but workers are not taxed on the value of the fringes. Consequently, fringes have a big advantage over cash wages. As taxation has become heavier and heavier, fringes have become more and more important in the total package offered by employers to workers—fringes were only 1.2 percent of total compensation in 1929, when income taxes were unimportant, but reached almost 18 percent in 1993. The explosion of fringes is strictly an artifact of taxation and thus an economically inefficient way to pay workers. Were the tax system neutral, with equal taxes on fringes and cash, workers would rather take their income in cash and make their own decisions about health and life insurance, parking, exercise facilities, and all the other things they now get from their employers without much choice. Further, failing to tax fringes means that taxes on other types of income are all the higher. Bringing all types of income under the tax system is essential for low rates.

Under our system, each business would file a simple form. Even the largest business (General Motors Corporation in 1993, with $138 billion in sales) would fill out our simple postcard form. Every line on the form is a well-defined number obtained directly from the business's accounting records. Line 1, gross revenue from sales, is the actual number of dollars received from the sales of all the products and services sold by the business, plus the proceeds from the sale of plant, equipment, and land. Line 2a is the actual amount paid for all the inputs bought from other businesses for the operation of the business (that is, not passed on to its workers or owners). The firm could report any purchase provided the purchase was for the business's operations and not part of the compensation of workers or owners. Line 2b is the actual cash put in the hands of workers and

former workers. All the dollars deducted on this line will
have to be reported by the workers on their Form 1
wage-tax returns. Line 2c reports purchases of new and
used capital equipment, buildings, and land. Note that
the firm won't have to agonize over whether a screw-
driver is a capital investment or a current input—both
are deductible, and the IRS won't care which line it will
appear on.

The taxable income computed on line 4 bears little
resemblance to anyone's notion of profit. The business
tax is not a profit tax. When a company is having an
outstanding year in sales and profits but is building new
factories to handle rapid growth, it may well have a low
or even negative taxable income. That's fine—later,
when expansion slows but sales are at a high level, the
income generated will be taxed at 19 percent.

Because the business tax treats investment in plant,
equipment, and land as an expense, companies in the
start-up period will have negative taxable income. But
the government will not write a check for the negative
tax on the negative income. Whenever the government
has a policy of writing checks, clever people abuse the
opportunity. Instead, the negative tax would be carried
forward to future years, when the business should have
a positive taxable income. There is no limit to the number of years of carry forward. Moreover, balances carried
forward will earn the market rate of interest (6 percent
in 1995). Lines 6 through 10 show the mechanics of
the carry-forward process.

Examples

The easiest way to explain how the business tax operates is through some examples. Our first example is the company with the highest level of revenue in 1993, General Motors (see figure 3.3; in this and other examples of real businesses, we have approximated the numbers from public financial statements for 1993).

Despite the low 19 percent flat tax, it would raise considerably more revenue than General Motors (GM) actually paid at the current 35 percent rate. (In 1993, GM actually paid about $110,000,000 in income taxes.) The main reason is that GM has a large amount of debt—the company paid out $5.7 billion in interest in 1993. The flat tax collects the tax on that amount from GM, instead of trying to collect it from the thousands of organizations and people who receive it. A second reason the flat tax generates more revenue is that GM invested relatively little in 1993, only about $6 billion. Under the current tax, GM wrote off over $9 billion in depreciation deductions for past investment.

Now look at the return for Intel Corporation (see figure 3.4). Because Intel is investing and growing rapidly, its taxes would be low and it would benefit tremendously from the first-year write-off for investment.

Intel's actual income tax in 1993 was $1.2 billion. The flat tax is lower for three reasons:

- The flat-tax rate of 19 percent is much lower than the current rate of 35 percent.
- Unlike GM, Intel has no debt, so the switch to

Form 2	Business Tax	1998
Business name General Motors		Employer identification number 48-2665679
Street address 3044 W. Grand Blvd.		County Wayne
City, state, and ZIP code Detroit, Mi 48202		Principal product Automobiles

1 Gross revenue from sales	1	138,219,500,000
2 Allowable costs		
(a) Purchases of goods, services, and materials	2(a)	53,210,950,000
(b) Wages, salaries, and pensions	2(b)	64,742,850,000
(c) Purchases of capital equipment, structures, and land	2(c)	5,935,800,000
3 Total allowable costs (sum of lines 2(a), 2(b), 2(c))	3	123,889,600,000
4 Taxable income (line 1 less line 3)	4	14,329,900,000
5 Tax (19% of line 4)	5	2,722,681,000
6 Carry-forward from 1997	6	0
7 Interest on carry-forward (6% of line 6)	7	0
8 Carry-forward into 1998 (line 6 plus line 7)	8	0
9 Tax due (line 5 less line 8, if positive)	9	2,722,681,000
10 Carry-forward to 1999 (line 8 less line 5, if positive)	10	0

Figure 3.3 General Motors' Business-Tax Form

Form 2		Business Tax		1998
Business name Intel Corporation			Employer identification number 96-8496331	
Street address P.O. Box 58119			County Santa Clara	
City, state, and ZIP code Santa Clara, CA 95052			Principal product Semiconductors	
1 Gross revenue from sales...	1		8,782,000,000	
2 Allowable costs				
(a) Purchases of goods, services, and materials..................	2(a)		1,626,000,000	
(b) Wages, salaries, and pensions....................................	2(b)		2,764,000,000	
(c) Purchases of capital equipment, structures, and land.......	2(c)		1,933,000,000	
3 Total allowable costs (*sum of lines 2(a), 2(b), 2(c)*).............	3		7,323,000,000	
4 Taxable income (*line 1 less line 3*).................................	4		1,459,000,000	
5 Tax (*19% of line 4*)...	5		277,000,000	
6 Carry-forward from 1997..	6		0	
7 Interest on carry-forward (*6% of line 6*)..........................	7		0	
8 Carry-forward into 1998 (*line 6 plus line 7*).....................	8		0	
9 Tax due (*line 5 less line 8, if positive*)............................	9		277,000,000	
10 Carry-forward to 1999 (*line 8 less line 5, if positive*)........	10		0	

Figure 3.4 Intel Corporation's Business-Tax Form

source taxation for interest does not raise extra revenue from Intel the way it did for GM.

• Intel is investing heavily in new plant and equipment.

Now let's look at some smaller businesses and activities that would be taxed under the business tax, even
though they may not usually be called businesses. Sigrid
Seigneur and Sanford Seigneur are a prosperous couple
who bought an apartment building a few years ago. Assuming that the business tax had been in effect from the
year they bought the building, their 1995 tax return
would look like the form we have included here (see
figure 3.5). The gross revenue the couple would report
is just the total of the rent paid by their tenants. Their
costs include the payments to the plumber for the frozen
pipe in February 1995, the insurance premiums, and a
handful of other expenses. Neither the interest on the
mortgage they have on the property nor their property
tax bills would be counted as costs. Their tax for 1995,
$11,563, would be substantial, but the large carry for-
ward from the purchase of the building means they
would not pay anything in 1995. As time goes by, the
carry forward will probably decline (depending on what
happens to rents and interest rates), and they will begin
to pay tax. If they sell the building, they will have to
include the proceeds of the sale on line 1 and pay 19
percent of the sale price, minus any remaining carry
forward.

Seymour Krankheit is a successful pediatric neuro-
surgeon. His gross revenue under the flat tax would be

Form 2		Business Tax		1998

Business name
Sanford and Sigrid Seigneur

Employer identification number
14-08041

Street address
435 Riverside Drive

City, state, and ZIP code
Atchison, Kansas 10832

County
Atchison

Principal product
Apartment rentals

1 Gross revenue from sales..	**1**	68,323
2 Allowable costs		
(a) Purchases of goods, services, and materials...................	**2(a)**	7,467
(b) Wages, salaries, and pensions..	**2(b)**	0
(c) Purchases of capital equipment, structures, and land......	**2(c)**	0
3 Total allowable costs (sum of lines 2(a), 2(b), 2(c))...............	**3**	7,467
4 Taxable income (line 1 less line 3)..	**4**	60,856
5 Tax (19% of line 4)...	**5**	11,563
6 Carry-forward from 1997...	**6**	37,892
7 Interest on carry-forward (6% of line 6)...................................	**7**	2,274
8 Carry-forward into 1998 (line 6 plus line 7)............................	**8**	40,166
9 Tax due (line 5 less line 8, if positive)....................................	**9**	0
10 Carry-forward to 1999 (line 8 less line 5, if positive)............	**10**	28,603

Figure 3.5 Sigrid Seigneur and Sanford Seigneur's Business-Tax Form

the amount he collects from insurance companies, Medicare, Medicaid, and the occasional unlucky family who pays its own medical bills. He also receives a salary as a hospital employee, but that income would be reported on his wage-tax return (see figure 3.1). All the costs of running his office would be included in allowable costs, except the fringe benefits he provides his nurse and himself. Under the present tax system, as a professional corporation, he can deduct tens of thousands of dollars as contributions to his own pension plan, but the flat-tax reform would eliminate that deduction. He could still be a professional corporation if he wanted, but it wouldn't have any tax advantages. Even though he is in the 40 percent bracket under the current personal income tax and under the flat tax will pay only 19 percent, he would actually pay more dollars of tax under our system (see figure 3.6).

Although Dr. Krankheit can't set up a retirement plan and deduct contributions to it, he, along with everyone else, can get the same economic advantages that a retirement plan currently provides. If he sets aside some of his income after tax and puts it into a mutual fund, he will not pay any tax on the mutual fund's earnings and he can spend his mutual fund balance after he retires, without paying any more tax. Under the current tax, he gets a tax deduction up front but has to pay tax on the entire amount he takes out when he retires. These two approaches differ only in the timing of the tax payment; they are economically equivalent because the accumulated earnings make the later tax payment in the current system enough larger than the up-front

Form 2	Business Tax		1998
Business name Seymour Krankheit, MD			Employer identification number 97-01469
Street address 1948 Prospect Road			County Dallas
City, state, and ZIP code Dallas, Texas 83045			Principal product Medical Services
1 Gross revenue from sales..	**1**		567,163
2 Allowable costs			
(a) Purchases of goods, services, and materials.................	**2(a)**	87,997	
(b) Wages, salaries, and pensions.................................	**2(b)**	55,874	
(c) Purchases of capital equipment, structures, and land......	**2(c)**	36,448	
3 Total allowable costs (sum of lines 2(a), 2(b), 2(c))............	**3**		180,319
4 Taxable income (line 1 less line 3)...............................	**4**		386,844
5 Tax (19% of line 4)...	**5**		73,500
6 Carry-forward from 1997...	**6**		0
7 Interest on carry-forward (6% of line 6).........................	**7**		0
8 Carry-forward into 1998 (line 6 plus line 7).....................	**8**		0
9 Tax due (line 5 less line 8, if positive)..........................	**9**		73,500
10 Carry-forward to 1999 (line 8 less line 5, if positive).........	**10**		0

Figure 3.6 Dr. Krankheit's Business-Tax Form

payment under the flat tax to exactly offset the time value of money.

Our third example, Sally Vendeuse, works as a manufacturers' representative—she is a traveling saleswoman. Her gross revenue on line 1 consists of the commissions she earns (see figure 3.7). Her allowable costs would include all of her travel expenses and the costs of taking her customers to lunch. On line 3c, she would deduct the full cost of a car she bought for business use. She could have paid herself a salary of any amount she chose. If she were single, she would want to pay herself at least $9,500 to take advantage of the personal allowance in the wage tax, but her husband earns a salary as a teacher, so there would be no benefit to paying herself a salary.

Samuel Agricola is a farmer in Iowa (see figure 3.8). His gross revenue would be the total amount he receives from the sale of the corn and other crops he grows. In 1995 it fell a little short of what he paid to his suppliers and workers, so the government would let him take the $4,459 carry forward against future taxes, when the normal profitability of the farm returns.

INVESTMENT INCENTIVES

Almost all experts agree that the high rates of the current tax system significantly impede capital formation. The government's solution to the problem has been to pile one special investment or saving incentive on top of another, creating a complex and unworkable maze of regulations and tax forms. Existing incentives are ap-

Form 2	Business Tax		1998

Business name
Sally Vendeuse

Employer identification number
15-13255

Street address
903 S. Ashland

County
Lancaster

City, state, and ZIP code
Lancaster, PA 02351

Principal product
Sales services

1 Gross revenue from sales	**1**	101,008
2 Allowable costs		
(a) Purchases of goods, services, and materials	**2(a)**	12,896
(b) Wages, salaries, and pensions	**2(b)**	0
(c) Purchases of capital equipment, structures, and land	**2(c)**	27,445
3 Total allowable costs (sum of lines 2(a), 2(b), 2(c))	**3**	40,341
4 Taxable income (line 1 less line 3)	**4**	60,667
5 Tax (19% of line 4)	**5**	11,527
6 Carry-forward from 1997	**6**	0
7 Interest on carry-forward (6% of line 6)	**7**	0
8 Carry-forward into 1998 (line 6 plus line 7)	**8**	0
9 Tax due (line 5 less line 8, if positive)	**9**	11,527
10 Carry-forward to 1999 (line 8 less line 5, if positive)	**10**	0

Figure 3.7 Sally Vendeuse's Business-Tax Form

Form 2	Business Tax		1998
Business name Samuel Agricola		Employer identification number 53-89617	
Street address Rural Route 2		County Keokuk	
City, state, and ZIP code Gibson City, Iowa 60436		Principal product Corn	
1 Gross revenue from sales...	1		347,872
2 Allowable costs			
(a) Purchases of goods, services, and materials..................	2(a)	197,357	
(b) Wages, salaries, and pensions....................................	2(b)	107,490	
(c) Purchases of capital equipment, structures, and land.......	2(c)	66,496	
3 Total allowable costs (sum of lines 2(a), 2(b), 2(c)).............	3	371,343	
4 Taxable income (line 1 less line 3)..................................	4		-23,471
5 Tax (19% of line 4)..	5		-4,459
6 Carry-forward from 1997..	6		0
7 Interest on carry-forward (6% of line 6)...........................	7		0
8 Carry-forward into 1998 (line 6 plus line 7)......................	8		0
9 Tax due (line 5 less line 8, if positive).............................	9		0
10 Carry-forward to 1999 (line 8 less line 5, if positive)..........	10		4,459

Figure 3.8 Samuel Agricola's Business-Tax Form

pallingly uneven. Capital projects taking full advantage
of depreciation deductions and the deductibility of interest paid to organizations exempt from income tax may
actually receive subsidies from the government, rather
than being taxed. But equity-financed projects are heavily taxed. Investment incentives severely distort the flow
of capital into projects eligible for debt finance.

Our idea is to start over, throwing away all the present incentives and replacing them with a simple, uniform principle—treating the total amount of investment
as an expense in the year it is made. The entire incentive for capital formation is on the investment side, instead of the badly fitting split in the current tax system
between investment incentives and saving incentives.
The first virtue of this reform is simplicity. Businesses
and government need not quarrel, as they do now, over
what is an investment and what is a current expense.
The distinction doesn't matter for the flat tax. Complicated depreciation calculations, carrying over from one
year to the next and driving the small-business owner to
distraction, will vanish from the tax form. The even
more complicated provisions for recapturing depreciation when a piece of equipment or a building is sold
will vanish as well, to everyone's relief.

Expensing investment has a much deeper rationale
than simplicity. Every act of investment in the economy
ultimately traces back to an act of saving. A tax on income with an exemption for saving is in effect a tax on
consumption, for consumption is the difference between income and saving. Consumption is what people
take out of the economy; income is what people con-

tribute. A consumption tax is the exact embodiment of the principle that people should be taxed on what they take out, not what they put in. The flat tax, by expensing investment, is precisely a consumption tax.

Expensing investment eliminates the double taxation of saving, another way to express the most economically significant feature of expensing. Under an income tax, people pay tax once when they earn and save and again when the savings earn a return. With expensing, the first tax is abolished. Saving is, in effect, deducted in computing the tax. Later, the return to the saving is taxed through the business tax. Although economists have dreamt up a number of ways to eliminate double taxation of saving (involving complicated record keeping and reporting by individuals), the technique exploited in our flat tax is by far the most straightforward.

The easiest way to show that expensing investment is a consumption tax arises when someone invests directly in a personally owned business. Suppose a taxpayer receives $1,000 in earnings and turns around and buys a piece of business equipment for $1,000. Under the flat tax, there is a tax of $190 on the earnings but also a deduction worth $190 in reduced taxes for the equipment purchase. On net, there is no tax. The taxpayer has not consumed any of the original $1,000. Later the taxpayer will receive business income representing the earnings of the machine, which will be taxed at 19 percent. If the taxpayer chooses to consume rather than invest again, there will be a 19 percent tax on the consumption. So the overall effect is a 19 percent consumption tax.

Most people, however, don't invest by directly purchasing machines. The U.S. economy has wonderfully developed financial markets for channeling savings from individual savers to businesses who have good investment opportunities. Individuals invest by purchasing shares or bonds, and the firms then purchase plant and equipment. The tax system we propose taxes the consumption of individuals in this environment as well. Suppose the same taxpayer pays the $190 tax on the same $1,000 and puts the remaining $810 into the stock market. For simplicity, suppose that the share pays out to its owner all the after-tax earnings on equipment costing $1,000. (That assumption makes sense because the firm could buy $1,000 worth of equipment with the $810 from our taxpayer plus the tax write-off worth $190 that would come with the equipment purchase.) Our taxpayer gets the advantage of the investment write-off even though there is no deduction for purchasing the share. The market passes the incentive from the firm on to the individual investor.

Another possibility for the taxpayer is to buy a bond for $810. Again, the firm issuing the bond can buy a $1,000 machine with the $810, after taking advantage of the tax deduction. To compete with the returns available in the stock market, however, the bond must pay the same returns as a stock selling for the same price, which in turn is equal to the after-tax earnings of the machine, so it won't matter how the taxpayer invests the $810. In all cases, there is effectively no tax for saved income; the tax is payable only when the income is consumed.

In our system, any investment, in effect, would have the same economic advantage that a 401(k), IRA, or Keogh account has in the current tax system. And we achieve this desirable goal by reducing the amount of record keeping and reporting. Today, taxpayers have to deduct their Keogh-IRA contributions on their Form 1040s and then report the distributions from the funds as income when they retire. Moreover, proponents of the cash-flow consumption tax would extend these requirements to all forms of saving. Our system would accomplish the same goal without any forms or record keeping.

CAPITAL GAINS

Capital gains on rental property, plant, and equipment would be taxed under the business tax. The purchase price would be deducted at the time of purchase, and the sale price would be taxed at the time of the sale. Every owner of rental real estate would be required to fill out the simple business- tax return, Form 2 (figure 3.2).

Capital gains would be taxed exclusively at the business level, not at the personal level. In other words, our system would eliminate the double taxation of capital gains inherent in the current tax system. To see how this works, consider the common stock of a corporation. The market value of the stock is the capitalization of its future earnings. Because the owners of the stock will receive their earnings after the corporation has paid the business tax, the market capitalizes after-tax earnings. A capital gain occurs when the market perceives that prospective after-tax earnings have risen. When the higher earnings materialize in the future, they will be correspondingly taxed. In a tax system like the current one, with both an income tax and a capital gains tax, there is double taxation. To achieve the goal of taxing all income exactly once, the best answer is to place an airtight tax on the income at the source. With taxation at the source, it is inappropriate and inefficient to tax capital gains that occur at the destination.

Another way to see that capital gains should not be taxed separately is to look at the national income accounts. Gross domestic product, the most comprehensive measure of the nation's command over resources, does not include capital gains. The base of the flat tax is GDP minus investment, that is, consumption. To include capital gains in the flat-tax base would depart from the principle that it is a tax on consumption.

Capital gains on owner-occupied houses are not taxed under our proposal. Few capital gains on houses are taxed under the current system—gains can be rolled over, there is an exclusion for older home sellers, and gains are never taxed at death. Excluding capital gains on houses makes sense because state and local governments put substantial property taxes on houses in relation to their values. Adding a capital gains tax on top of property taxes is double taxation in the same way that adding a capital gains tax on top of an income tax is double taxation of business income.

BANKS AND INSURANCE COMPANIES

Banks, insurance companies, and other businesses that bundle services with financial products present a challenge to any tax system. Here is the problem: Suppose a depositor has a balance of $1,000 in a personal account, averaged over the year. At market interest rates, the depositor should earn at least $40 in interest, and this interest income would be taxable. But the bank bundles services with the basic function of borrowing from the depositor and offsets the price of the services against interest payments. The services include processing deposits, clearing checks, preparing statements, providing automatic teller services, and even free safe deposit boxes. By deducting the prices of the services and paying only the remainder as interest, the bank is, in effect, letting the depositor deduct the prices of the services. The government is the loser. Proper accounting would require that the depositor report the entire amount of interest as income and not deduct the prices of the services. Note that this problem only arises when the depositor is not a business—a business would be entitled to deduct the prices of the services.

At first, it may seem that the flat tax would solve this problem effortlessly. The interest the bank pays its depositors would not be taxed under our system. But the problem arises in another place—the application of the business tax to the bank itself. Take a simple example, a bank that bundles so many attractive services that none of its accounts pay any interest. The bank invests all its depositors' money in bonds. The bank would have no revenue on line 1 of its business-tax Form 2. Remember that line 1 reports income from the sale of goods and services and does not include financial income. The bank would report, however, all the costs of providing its services on lines 2a, 2b, and 2c—paper, computer services, wages and salaries, and purchases of equipment. The bank would appear to operate at a loss year after year. In the case of an actual bank, which does sell services to its customers, the problem would still exist, though it would be less conspicuous. A bank would appear to generate less taxable income that it really does, as a result of bundled services.

Banks are a problem in any tax system. The solution is to require that banks report the price of the services they provide to depositors. The price is easy to measure—it is the difference between the market interest rate and the lower rate that the bank pays on accounts that have bundled services. For example, when the interest rate on Treasury bills is 5 percent and checking accounts are paying 2 percent, the price of the bundled services is the difference, 3 percent of the balance in the account. Line 1 on a bank's Form 2 should include the valuation of all bundled services on this principle.

Bank loans present a similar challenge. A loan is actually a financial transaction bundled with services provided by the bank. The value of the services generates about a 3 percentage point margin between the pure interest rate and the lending rate. Again, line 1 of a bank's Form 2 should include the value of services associated with loans.

Our last example is Form 2 for the First National

Bank of Rocky Mount, Virginia (see figure 3.9). The profit-and-loss statement for the bank shows only $452,000 in income other than interest income. But after imputing 0.80 percentage points of service value to all its deposits (other than very large certificates of deposit that are essentially purely financial instruments) and 2.98 percentage points of service value to its loans, its income is $4,660,000 in total. Its flat tax of $259,000 is below its actual 1993 tax of $471,000, mainly because of the lower rate.

Taxation of life insurance companies should follow the same principle—they should report extra income on line 1 of Form 2 whenever they pay less than the market rate of interest to their policyholders.

The principle appears in our proposed flat-tax law in a general way: Under the business tax, the revenue from any service provided in connection with a financial transaction must be augmented by the difference between the market interest rate and the actual rate paid as part of the transaction.

IMPORTS, EXPORTS, AND MULTINATIONAL BUSINESS

With the North American Free Trade Agreement and the growth of trade throughout the world, U.S. companies are doing more business in other countries and foreign companies are increasingly active here. Should the U.S. government try to tax American-owned business operations in other countries? Should it tax foreign operations in the United States? These are increasingly

Form 2	Business Tax		1998
Business name First National Bank of Rocky Mount		Employer identification number 54-0962185	
Street address 249 Franklin Street		County Franklin County	
City, state, and ZIP code Rocky Mount, VA 24151		Principal product Banking	
1 Gross revenue from sales...	1		4,660,000
2 Allowable costs			
(a) Purchases of goods, services, and materials............	2(a)		974,100
(b) Wages, salaries, and pensions..................................	2(b)		2,272,900
(c) Purchases of capital equipment, structures, and land....	2(c)		52,000
3 Total allowable costs *(sum of lines 2(a), 2(b), 2(c))*...........	3		3,299,000
4 Taxable income *(line 1 less line 3)*..................................	4		1,361,000
5 Tax *(19% of line 4)*..	5		258,590
6 Carry-forward from 1997..	6		0
7 Interest on carry-forward *(6% of line 6)*..........................	7		0
8 Carry-forward into 1998 *(line 6 plus line 7)*.....................	8		0
9 Tax due *(line 5 less line 8, if positive)*............................	9		258,590
10 Carry-forward to 1999 *(line 8 less line 5, if positive)*........	10		0

Figure 3.9 First National's Business-Tax Form

controversial questions. Under the current tax system, foreign operations of U.S. companies are taxed in principle, but the taxpayer receives a credit against U.S. taxes for taxes paid to the country where the business operates. Because the current tax system is based on a confused combination of taxing some income at the origin and some at the destination, taxation of foreign operations is messy.

By consistently taxing all business income at the source, the flat tax embodies a clean solution to the problems of multinational operations. The flat tax applies only to the domestic operations of all businesses, whether of domestic, foreign, or mixed ownership. Only the revenue from the sales of products within the United States plus the value of products as they are exported would be reported on line 1 of the business-tax Form 2. Only the costs of labor, materials, and other inputs purchased in the United States or imported to the United States would be allowable on line 2 as deductions for the business tax. Physical presence in the United States is the simple rule that determines whether a purchase or sale is included in taxable revenue or allowable cost.

To see how the business tax would apply to foreign trade, consider first an importer selling its wares within the United States. Its costs would include the actual amount it paid for its imports, valued as they entered the country (this would generally be the actual amount paid for them in the country of their origin). Its revenue would be the actual receipts from sales in the United States. Second, consider an exporter selling goods produced here to foreigners. Its costs would be all the in-

puts and compensation paid in the United States, and
its revenue would be the amount received from sales to
foreigners, provided that the firm did not add to the
product after it departed the country. Third, consider a
firm that sends parts to Mexico for assembly and brings
back the final product for sale in the United States. The
value of the parts as they leave here would count as part
of the revenue of the firm, and the value of the assembled product when it was returned would be an expense.
The firm would not deduct the actual costs of its Mex-
ican assembly plant.

Under the principle of only taxing domestic activities, the U.S. tax system would mesh neatly with the tax
systems of our major trading partners. If every nation
used the flat tax, all income throughout the world would
be taxed once and only once. Because the basic principle of the flat tax is already in use in the many nations
with value-added taxes, a U.S. flat tax would harmonize
nicely with those foreign tax systems.

Application of the wage tax, Form 1 (figure 3.1), in
the world economy would follow the same principle.
All earnings from work in the United States would be
taxed, irrespective of the worker's citizenship, but the
tax would not apply to the foreign earnings of Americans.

Choices about the international location of businesses and employment are influenced by differences in
tax rates. The United States, with a low tax rate of 19
percent, would be much the most attractive location
among major industrial nations from the point of view
of taxation. Although the flat tax would not tax the over-

seas earnings of American workers and businesses, there is no reason to fear an exodus of economic activity. On the contrary, the favorable tax climate in the United States would draw in new business from everywhere in the world.

SOCIAL SECURITY

We are not disposed to tackle in this book the enormous topic of reforming the Social Security system. The Social Security tax is second only to the personal income tax in federal revenues, but we have not made proposals for changing that tax. It is worth pointing out, however, that the Social Security tax is a completely successful flat tax—since its inception in the 1930s, it has remained remarkably free from complicating amendments. Its history shows that we are perfectly capable of keeping a tax flat.

The interaction of Social Security with the flat tax would work in the following way: The employer's contribution would be treated like other fringe benefits—it would not be deductible from the business tax. Here we are departing from the existing system, where the employer's contribution is deductible. As at present, the employee's contribution would be included in taxable income under the wage tax. Social Security benefits would be completely untaxed. We would eliminate the current partial taxation of benefits for higher-income taxpayers. Eliminating the employer's deduction for contributions is a better way to tax benefits.

In this book, the bulk of our effort is devoted to laying out a good, practical tax system, and we have not made concessions to the political pressures that may well force the nation to accept an improved tax system that falls short of our ideal. One area where the political process is likely to complicate our simple proposal is the transition from the current tax to the flat tax, with the most attention drawn to depreciation and interest deductions. In both cases, taxpayers who made plans and commitments before the tax reform will cry loudly for special provisions to continue the deductions.

Congress will face a choice between denying taxpayers the deductions they expected before tax reform or granting the deductions and raising the tax rate to make up for the lost revenue. Fortunately, this is a temporary problem. Once existing capital is fully depreciated and the existing borrowing paid off, any special transition provisions can be taken off the books.

Depreciation Deductions

Existing law lets businesses deduct the cost of an investment on a declining schedule over many years. From the point of view of the business, multiyear depreciation deductions are not as attractive as the first-year write-off prescribed in the flat tax. No business will complain about the flat tax as far as future investment is concerned. But businesses may well protest the unexpected elimination of the unused depreciation they thought they would be able to take on the plant and equipment they installed before the tax reform. Without special transition provisions, these deductions would simply be lost.

How much is at stake? In 1992, total depreciation deductions under the personal and corporate income taxes came to $597 billion. At the 35 percent rate for most corporations (which is close to the rate paid by the individuals who are likely to take deductions as proprietors or partners), those deductions were worth $209 billion. At the 19 percent flat rate, the deductions would be worth only $108 billion.

If Congress chose to honor all unused depreciation from investment predating tax reform, it would take about $597 billion out of the tax base for 1995. To raise the same amount of revenue as our 19 percent rate, the tax rate would have to rise to about 20.1 percent.

Honoring past depreciation would mollify business interests, especially in industries with large amounts of unused depreciation for past investment but little prospect of large first-year write-offs for future investment. In addition, it would buttress the government's credibility in tax matters by carrying through on a past promise to give a tax incentive for investment. In contrast, however, the move would require a higher tax rate and a less efficient economy in the future.

If Congress did opt to honor past depreciation, it should recognize that the higher tax rate needed to make up for the lost revenue is temporary. Within five years, the bulk of the existing capital would be depreciated and the tax rate should be brought back to 19 percent. From the outset, the tax rate should be committed to drop to 19 percent as soon as the transition depreciation is paid off.

Interest Deductions

Loss of interest deductions and eliminating interest taxation are two of the most conspicuous features of our tax reform plan. We will discuss the important economic changes that would take place once interest is put on an after-tax basis in the next chapter. During the transition, there will be winners and losers from the change, and Congress is sure to hear from the losers. Congress may well decide to adopt a temporary transitional measure to help them. Such a measure need not compromise the principles of the flat tax or lessen its contribution to improved efficiency.

Our tax reform calls for the parallel removal of interest deduction and interest taxation. If a transitional measure allows deductions for interest on outstanding debt, it should also require taxation of that interest as income of the lender. If all deductions are completely matched with taxation on the other side, then a transition provision to protect existing interest deductions would have no effect on revenue. In that respect, interest deductions are easier to handle in the transition than depreciation deductions.

If Congress decides that a transitional measure to protect interest deductions is needed, we suggest the following. Any borrower may choose to treat interest payments as a tax deduction. If the borrower so chooses, the lender must treat the interest as taxable income. But the borrower's deduction should be only 90 percent of the actual interest payment, while the lender's taxable income should include 100 percent of the interest receipts.

Under this transitional plan, borrowers would be protected for almost all their existing deductions. Someone whose personal finances would become untenable if the mortgage-interest deduction were suddenly eliminated can surely get through with 90 percent of the earlier deduction. But the plan builds in an incentive for renegotiating the interest payments along the lines we discussed earlier in this chapter. Suppose a family is paying $10,000 in annual mortgage interest. It could stick with this payment and deduct $9,000 per year. Its net cost, after subtracting the value of its deduction with the 19 percent tax rate, would be $8,290. The net income to the bank, after subtracting the 19 percent tax it pays on the whole $10,000, would be $8,100. Alternatively, the family could accept a deal proposed by the bank: The interest payment would be lowered to $8,200 by rewriting the mortgage. The family would agree to forgo its right to deduct the interest, and the bank would no longer have to pay tax on the interest. Now the family's cost will be $8,200 (instead of $8,290 without the deal), and the bank's income will be $8,200 (instead of $8,100 without the deal). The family will come out $90 ahead, and the bank will come out $100 ahead. The deal will be beneficial to both.

One of the nice features of this plan is that it does not make any distinctions between old borrowing, existing at the time of the tax reform, and new borrowing, arranged after the reform. Lenders would always require that new borrowers opt out of their deductions and thus would offer a correspondingly lower interest rate. Otherwise, the lender would be saddled with a tax bill larger than the tax deduction received by the borrower.

As far as revenue is concerned, this plan would actually add a bit to federal revenue in comparison to the pure flat tax. Whenever a borrower exercised the right to deduct interest, the government would collect more revenue from the lender than it would lose from the borrower. As more and more deals were rewritten to eliminate deductions and lower interest, the excess revenue would disappear and we would be left with the pure flat tax.

VARIANTS OF THE FLAT TAX

In this chapter, we have set forth what we think is the best flat tax. But our ideas are more general than this specific proposal. The same principles could be applied with different choices about the key trade-offs. The two most important trade-offs are

- *Progressivity versus tax rate.* A higher personal allowance would put an even lower burden on low- and middle-income families. But it would require a higher tax rate.

- *Investment incentives versus tax rate.* If the business tax had less than full write-off for purchases of capital goods, the tax rate could be lower.

Here are some alternative combinations of allowances and tax rates that would raise the same amount
of revenue:

Allowance for Family of Four	Tax Rate
$12,500	15%
22,500	19%
34,500	23%

The choice among these alternatives depends on
beliefs about how the burden of taxes should be distributed and on the degree of inefficiency that will be
brought into the economy by the corresponding tax
rates. We will have more to say about the inefficiency
issue in the next chapter.

Here are some alternative combinations of investment write-offs and tax rates that would raise the same
amount of revenue:

Equipment Write-Off	Structures Write-Off	Tax Rate
100%	100%	19%
75%	50%	18%
50%	25%	17%

The choice among these alternatives depends on
the sensitivity of investment/saving to incentives and on
the degree of inefficiency brought by the tax rate.

4. The Flat Tax and the Economy

TAX REFORM ALONG the lines of our simple tax will influence the American economy profoundly: Improved incentives for work, entrepreneurial activity, and capital formation will substantially raise national output and the standard of living. Everyone would favor such an economic renaissance. But what about some of the other effects of tax reform? Is it a giveaway to the rich? Will it destroy the housing market by ending mortgage deductions? Can charitable institutions survive without tax deductions for gifts? Can the flat tax end the federal deficit? These questions have occurred to almost everyone who ponders our radical reform, and we take those questions seriously. This chapter tries to take an honest look at those major economic issues.

STIMULUS TO GROWTH

The flat tax, at a low, uniform rate of 19 percent, will improve the performance of the U.S. economy. Improved incentives to work through increased take-home wages will stimulate work effort and raise total output. Rational investment incentives will raise the overall level of investment and channel it into the most productive areas. And sharply lower taxes on entrepreneurial effort will enhance this critical input to the economy.

Work Effort

About two-thirds of today's taxpayers enjoy the low income tax rate of 15 percent enacted in 1986. Under the
flat tax, more than half of these taxpayers would face
zero tax rates because their total family earnings would
fall short of the exemption amount ($25,500 for a family
of four). The other half would face a slight increase in
their tax rate on the margin, from 15 percent to 19 percent. In 1991, the remaining third of taxpayers were
taxed at rates of 28 and 31 percent, and the addition of
the 39.6 percent bracket in 1993 worsened incentives
further. Heavily taxed people earn a disproportionate
share of income: In 1991, 58 percent of all earnings
were taxed at rates of 28 percent or higher. The net
effect of the flat tax, with marginal rates of 0 and 19
percent, would be to dramatically improve incentives for
almost everyone who is economically active.

One point we need to emphasize is that a family's
marginal tax rate determines its incentives for all types
of economic activity, which has caused some confusion.
For example, some authors have written that married
women face a special disincentive because the marginal
tax on the first dollar of a married woman's earnings is
the same as the marginal tax on the last dollar of her
husband earnings. It is true that work incentives for a
woman with a well-paid husband are seriously eroded
by high tax rates. But so are her husband's incentives.
What matters to both of them is how much of any extra
dollar of earnings they will keep after taxes. Under the
U.S. income tax, with joint filing, the fraction either of

them takes home after taxes is always the same, no matter how their earnings are split between them.

Sheer hours of work make up one of the most important dimensions of productive effort and one that is known to be sensitive to incentives. At first, it may seem difficult for people to alter the amount of work they supply to the economy. Aren't most jobs forty hours a week, fifty-two weeks a year? It turns out that only a fraction of the workforce is restricted in that way. Most of us face genuine decisions about how much to work. Teenagers and young adults—in effect anyone before the responsibilities of parenthood—typically work much less than full time for the full year. Improving their incentives could easily make them switch from part-time to full-time work or cause them to spend less time taking it easy between jobs.

Married women remain one of the largest underutilized resources in the U.S. economy, although a growing fraction enters the labor market each year. In 1993, only 58 percent of all women over fifteen were at work or looking for work; the remaining 42 percent were spending their time at home or in school but could be drawn into the market if the incentives were right. There is no doubt about the sensitivity of married women to economic incentives. Studies show a systematic tendency for women with low after-tax wages and high-income husbands to work little. Those with high after-tax wages and lower-income husbands work a lot. It is thus reasonable to infer that sharply reduced marginal tax rates on married women's earnings will further stimulate their interest in the market.

Another remarkable source of unused labor power in the United States is men who have taken early retirement. Although 92 percent of men aged twenty-five to fifty-four are in the labor force, only 65 percent of those from fifty-five to sixty-four are at work or looking for work—just 17 percent of those over sixty-five. Again, retirement is a matter of incentives. High marginal taxes on earnings discourage many perfectly fit men from continuing to work. Because mature men are among the best paid in the economy, a great many of them face marginal tax rates of 28, 36, or even 40 percent. A uniform 19 percent rate could significantly reduce early retirement and make better use of the skills of older men.

Economists have devoted a great deal of effort to measuring the potential stimulus to work from tax reform. Their consensus is that all groups of workers would respond to the flat tax by raising their work effort. A few workers would reduce their hours either because the flat rate would exceed their current marginal rate or because the reform would add so much to their incomes that they would feel that earning was less urgent. But the great majority would face much improved incentives. The smallest responses are from adult men and the largest from married women.

In the light of the research on labor supply, were we to switch from the current tax law to our proposed flat tax, a reasonable projection is an increase of about 4 percent in total hours of work in the U.S. economy. That increase would mean about one and a half hours a week on average but would take the form of second jobs for some workers, more weeks of work a year for others, and more hours a week for those working part time. The total annual output of goods and services in the U.S. economy would rise by about 3 percent, or almost $200 billion. That is nearly $750 per person, an astonishing sum. Of course, it might take some time for the full influence of improved incentives to take effect. But the bottom line is unambiguous: Tax reform would have an important favorable effect on total work effort.

Capital Formation

Economists are far from agreement on the impact of tax reform on investment. As we stressed earlier, the existing system puts heavy tax rates on business income, even though the net revenue from the system is small. These rates seriously erode investment incentives. Erratic investment provisions in the current law and lax enforcement of taxes on business income at the personal level, however, combine to limit the adverse impact. The current tax system subsidizes investment through tax-favored entities such as pension funds, while taxing capital formation heavily if it takes the form of new businesses. The result has been to sustain capital formation at reasonably high levels but to channel the investment into inefficient uses.

The most important structural bias of the existing system is the double taxation of business income earned in corporations and paid out to shareholders. Double taxation dramatically reduces the incentive to create new businesses in risky lines where debt financing is not available. On the other side, the existing system places no current tax on investments that can be financed by debt and where the debt is held by pension funds or other nontaxed entities. The result is a huge twist in incentives, away from entrepreneurial activities and toward safe, debt-financed activities.

The flat tax would eliminate the harmful twist in the current tax system. The flat tax has a single, uniform incentive for investment of all types—businesses would treat all purchases of capital equipment and buildings as expenses. As we noted in the last chapter, allowing an immediate write-off of investment is the ideal investment incentive. A tax system that taxes all income evenly and allows expensing of investment is a tax on consumption. Public finance economists Alan Auerbach and Laurence Kotlikoff estimate that using a flat-rate consumption tax in place of an income tax would raise the ratio of capital stock to GDP from 5.0 to 6.2. Other economists are less optimistic that correcting the double taxation of saving would provide the resources for this large an increase in investment. But all agree that there would be *some* favorable effect on capital formation.

In terms of added GDP, the increase in the capital stock projected by Auerbach and Kotlikoff would translate into 6 percent more goods and services. Not all this extra growth would occur within the seven years after the flat tax goes into effect. But, even allowing for only partial attainment in seven years and for a possible overstatement in their work, it seems reasonable to predict a 2 to 4 percent increase in GDP on account of added capital formation within seven years.

Tax reform would improve the productivity of capital by directing investment to the most productive uses. Auerbach has demonstrated, in a paper published by the Brookings Institution, that the bias of the current tax system toward equipment and away from structures imposes a small but important burden on the economy. The flat tax would correct this bias. Auerbach estimates that the correction would be equivalent to a 3.2 percent increase in the capital stock. GNP would rise on this account by 0.8 percent.

Entrepreneurial Incentives and Effort

U.S. economic growth has slowed in the past two decades, and surely one reason is the confiscatory taxation of successful endeavors and the tax subsidy for safe, nonentrepreneurial undertakings. There are no scholarly studies with quantitative conclusions on the overall benefits from a fundamental shift, but they could be large.

Today's tax system punishes entrepreneurs. Part of the trouble comes from the interest deduction. The people in the driver's seat in the capital market, where money is loaned and borrowed, are those who lend out money on behalf of institutions and those individuals who have figured out how to avoid paying income tax on their interest. These people do not like to make loans to new businesses based on great new ideas. They do like making loans that are secured to readily marketable assets by mortgages or similar arrangements. It is easy to borrow from a pension fund to build an apartment building, buy a boxcar, put up a shopping center, or anything else where the fund can foreclose and sell the asset in case the borrower defaults. Funds will not lend money to entrepreneurs with new ideas because they are unable to evaluate what they could sell off in case of a default.

Entrepreneurs can and do raise money the hard way, by giving equity interests to investors. An active venture-capital market operates for exactly this purpose. But the cost to the entrepreneur is high—the ownership given to the financial backers deprives the entrepreneur of the full gain in case things work out well.

So far we have just described the harsh reality of trying to get other people to put money into a risky, innovative business. Even with the best tax system, or no taxes at all, entrepreneurs would not be able to borrow with ordinary bonds or loans and thus capture the entire future profits of a new business. Equity participation by investors is a fact of life. But the perverse tax system greatly worsens the incentives for entrepreneurs. The combination of corporate and personal taxation of equity investments is actually close to confiscation. The owners of a successful new business are taxed first when the profits flow in, at 34 percent, and again when the returns make their way to the entrepreneur and the other owners. All of them are likely to be in the 40 percent personal income tax bracket, making the combined effective tax rate close to 60 percent. The entrepreneur first gives a large piece of the action to the inactive owners who put up the capital and then surrenders well over half the remainder to the government.

The prospective entrepreneur will likely be attracted

to the easier life of the investor who uses borrowed money. How much easier it is to put up a shopping center, borrow from a pension fund or insurance company, and deduct everything paid to the inactive investor.

Today's absurd system taxes entrepreneurial success at 60 percent while actually subsidizing some leveraged investments. Our simple tax would put the same low rate on both activities. A huge redirection of national effort would follow that could only be good for national income. There is nothing wrong with shopping centers, apartment buildings, airplanes, boxcars, medical equipment, and cattle; but tax advantages have made us invest far too much in them, and their contribution to income is correspondingly low. Real growth will come when effort and capital flow back into innovation and the development of new businesses, the areas where confiscatory taxation has discouraged investment. The contribution to income from new resources will be correspondingly high.

Total Potential Growth from Improved Incentives

We project a 3 percent increase in output from increased total work in the U.S. economy and an additional increment to total output of 3 percent from added capital formation and dramatically improved entrepreneurial incentives. The sum of 6 percent is our best estimate of the improvement in real incomes after the economy has had seven years to assimilate the changed economic conditions brought about by the simple flat tax. Both the amount and the timing are conservative.

Even this limited claim for economic improvement represents enormous progress. By 2002, it would mean each American will have an income about $1,900 higher, in 1995 dollars, as a consequence of tax reform.

INCOME DISTRIBUTION AND FAIRNESS

The flat tax would not make everyone better off straightaway. Today, heavy taxation of successful salary earners and entrepreneurs yields quite a bit of revenue, pushing these people out of their most productive undertakings and diverting their attention to tax avoidance. Until a response to improved incentives takes place, the lower taxes on some people will have to be made up by higher taxes on others. If tax reform were a zero-sum process, giving relief to some by raising taxes on others, it would be unlikely to occur. Revitalizing the economy, with more income to divide between the big earners and the rest, is the point of tax reform. Our flat tax, however, is designed to be fair from the start. It will insulate the poor from all taxation and will dramatically limit the taxation of wages and salaries, especially among those who are most successful and productive. It will pay for these tax reductions by imposing a sensible tax at a low rate on business income, thus *raising* the amount of federal revenue collected from businesses.

Table 4.1   Comparison of Current Tax
and Flat Tax by Earnings

Earnings	Current Tax	Flat Tax
$7,800	$7	$0
12,500	157	0
17,500	567	0
22,500	1,346	525
27,500	2,020	1,483
35,000	3,027	2,894
44,500	4,375	4,758
60,000	7,338	7,734
85,000	12,786	12,475
130,000	23,554	21,028

Taxes on Wages and Salaries

We will now compare the current tax with the flat tax for families who have nothing but wage income; these comparisons are relevant for the great majority of Americans.

Table 4.1 shows the taxes that would have been paid under the 1991 personal income tax and under the flat-tax system (with the 1991 levels of personal allowances) by a married couple. (We have to go back to 1991 because it is the last year for which income tax data are available as we write.) At each earnings level, the current tax is the average amount of tax paid by married taxpayers with that income (defined as adjusted gross income). To calculate the flat tax that would have been paid by the typical family, we assumed that each family had 1.1 dependents, the actual average in 1991.

The table shows that people at every level of earnings will pay about the same or less under the flat wage tax than under the current personal income tax. Below about $10,000, neither tax system imposes any significant tax, in line with the national consensus that the poor should be excused from taxation. For earnings in the range of $10,000 to $30,000, the flat tax is substantially less than the current tax. The flat tax's generous allowances of $16,500 for a married couple plus $4,500 a child keep the middle-income tax burden at a low level. The flat tax is a little higher than the current income tax in the range from $30,000 to $90,000. For earnings of more than $100,000, the flat tax is lower because the current income tax has higher tax brackets that take effect in those income ranges.

Thus we see that high-salaried employees get a break under the flat tax in comparison to the current tax. Why do we advocate such a generous break for people who are well off? Incentives are the answer. To collect $23,554 from an individual with $130,000 in earnings, the 1991 system had to impose a marginal tax rate of 31 percent. For each dollar of extra pay for extra work, this person keeps only sixty-nine cents after income tax. Furthermore, even that high tax rate is no guarantee that anything like this much revenue will actually be collected from a family with this much salary. Remember that these computations refer to a family with no income apart from salary. In 1993, the situation was made worse by the addition of a new tax bracket with a 39.6 percent tax rate.

Recall that the flat-tax system will raise the same revenue as the current system. The individual wage tax component of the flat tax, however, will raise less revenue than the personal income tax, and, correspondingly, the business tax component of the flat tax will raise more revenue than the existing corporate income tax. Comparisons like the one we have just made are not the end of the story. For those families with interest, dividends, and other business income, we need to think about the taxes that they currently pay on that income under the present personal and corporate income taxes. We also need to think about the taxes they would pay under the flat business tax.

As we have stressed throughout this book, taxing business income under the present system is a complete mess. Despite the burdensome tax rates imposed on business income by the combination of the corporate and personal income taxes, the total amount of tax collected on business income is remarkably small. In 1991, revenue from the corporate income tax was only $98 billion. In addition, the tax paid on all nonwage income reported for the personal income tax was no more than $158 billion. Total revenue from business taxation was no more than $256 billion. By contrast, revenue from taxes on wages under the personal income tax was $290 billion. The average tax rate on business income (as defined for the flat tax) was 15.0 percent, and the average rate on wages was 10.4 percent.

The flat tax would put higher taxes on business income and lower taxes on wage income. The average tax rate on wages would be 8.5 percent (19 percent on the margin but less on the average because of the allowances). The average tax rate on business income would be exactly 19 percent. At 1991 levels, business tax revenue would rise from $256 billion under the present tax to $325 billion under the flat tax.

Ideally, we could calculate the impact of the shift to the flat tax on families with various levels of income. The wealthy family with large amounts of business income would pay more tax than at present because of the increase in the average tax rate from 15 percent to 19 percent. Unfortunately, we do not know much about the distribution of business income in the United States. A good deal but not all business income goes to the very rich. In that respect, a shift away from wage taxation and toward business taxation would be a progressive move.

Are there enough middle-income families with business income so that their total tax burden, counting both wage and business taxes, would rise after the shift to the flat tax? There is no way to tell. Data from income tax returns show a reasonable number of families whose reported incomes are in the range of $50,000 to $100,000 and who receive substantial business income. But we have no way of knowing how many of them are really middle income and how many are actually rich but have succeeded so well in understating their business income that they appear to be middle income.

There have to be quite a few families whose business incomes are grossly understated in their income tax returns. A total of $1,709 billion in business income was

INTEREST RATES

The flat tax would pull down interest rates immediately. Today's high interest rates are sustained partly by the income tax deduction for interest paid and the tax on interest earned. The tax benefit ameliorates much of the pain of high interest, and the IRS takes part of the income from interest. Borrowers tolerate high interest rates and lenders require them. The simple tax would permit no deduction for interest paid and put no tax on interest received. Interest payments throughout the economy will be flows of after-tax income, thanks to taxation of business income at the source.

With the flat tax, borrowers will no longer be so tolerant of interest payments and lenders will no longer be concerned about taxes. The meeting of minds in the credit market, where borrowing equals lending, will inevitably occur at a lower interest rate. Potentially, the fall could be spectacular. Much borrowing comes from corporations and wealthy individuals who face marginal tax rates of 34 and 40 percent. The wealthy, however, almost by definition, are the big lenders in the economy. If every lender and every borrower were in the 40 percent bracket, a tax reform eliminating deduction and taxation of interest would cut interest rates by four-tenths—for example, from 10 to 6 percent. But the leakage problem in the United States is so great that the actual drop in interest would be far short of this huge potential. So much lending comes through the devices by which the well-to-do get their interest income under low tax rates that a drop of four-tenths would be impos-

sible. Lenders taxed at low rates would be worse off if
taxation were eliminated but interest rates fell by that
much. In an economy with lenders enjoying low marginal rates before reform, the meeting of the minds
would have to come at an interest rate well above six-
tenths of the preform level. But the decline would be
at least a fifth—say from 10 percent to 8 percent. Reform would thus bring a noticeable drop in interest
rates.

One direct piece of evidence is municipal bonds,
which yield interest not taxed under the federal income
tax. Tax reform would make all bonds like tax-free municipals, so the current rates on municipals may tell us
something about the level of all interest rates after reform. In 1994, municipals yielded about one-sixth less
interest than comparable taxable bonds. But this is a
conservative measure of the likely fall in interest rates
after reform. Today, tax-free rates are kept high because
there are so many opportunities to own taxable bonds
in low-tax ways. Why buy a bond from the city of Los
Angeles paying 6 percent tax-free when you can create
a personal pension fund and buy a Pacific Telesis bond
paying 7 percent? Interest rates could easily fall to three-
quarters of their present levels after tax reform; rates on
tax-free securities would then fall a little as well.

The decline in interest rates brought about by putting interest on an after-tax basis would not by itself
change the economy very much. To Ford Motors, con-
templating borrowing to finance a modern plant, the
attraction of lower rates would be offset by the cost of
lost interest deductions. But the flat tax will do much

more than put interest on an after-tax basis. Tax rates on corporations will be slashed to a uniform 19 percent from the double taxation of a 34 percent corporate rate on top of a personal rate of up to 39.6 percent. And investment incentives will be improved through first-year write-off. All told, borrowing for investment purposes will become a better deal. As the likely investment boom develops, borrowing will rise and tend to push up interest rates. In principle, interest rates could rise to their prereform levels, but only if the boom is vigorous. We cannot be sure what will happen to interest rates after tax reform, but we can be sure that high-interest, low-investment stagnation will not occur. Either interest rates will fall or investment will take off.

As a safe working hypothesis, we will assume that interest rates fall in the year after tax reform by about a fifth, say from 10 to 8 percent. We assume a quiescent underlying economy, not perturbed by sudden shifts in monetary policy, government spending, or oil prices. Now, let us look at borrowing decisions before and after reform. Suppose a prereform entrepreneur is considering an investment yielding $1 million a year in revenue and involving $800,000 in interest costs at 10 percent interest. Today the entrepreneur pays a 40 percent tax on the net income of $200,000, giving an after-tax flow of $120,000. After reform, the entrepreneur will earn the same $1 million and pay $640,000 interest on the same principal at 8 percent. There will be a 19 percent tax on the earnings ($190,000), without deducting interest. After-tax income is $1,000,000 minus $640,000 minus $190,000, which equals $170,000, well above the

$120,000 before reform. Reform is to the entrepreneur's advantage and to the advantage of capital formation. Gains from the lower tax rate more than make up for losses from denial of the interest deduction.

How can it be that both the entrepreneur and the government come out ahead from the tax reform? They don't—there is one element missing from this accounting. Before the reform, the government collected some tax on the interest paid by the entrepreneur—potentially as much as 40 percent of the $800,000, but, as our stories about leakage make clear, the government is actually lucky to get a small fraction of that potential.

To summarize, the flat tax automatically lowers interest rates. Without an interest deduction, borrowers require lower costs. Without an interest tax, lenders are satisfied with lower payments. The simple flat tax will have an important effect on interest rates. Lower interest rates will also stimulate the housing market, a matter of concern to almost everyone.

Housing

Everyone who hears about the flat tax, with no deductions for interest, worries about its effect on the housing market. Won't eliminating the deduction depress the prices of existing houses and impoverish the homeowner who can only afford a house because of its interest deductions? Our answer to all of these questions is no, but we freely concede that there is a significant issue here.

In all but the long run, house prices are set by the demand for houses because the supply can only change slowly. If tax reform increases the cost of carrying a house of given value, then demand will fall and house prices will fall correspondingly. For this reason, we are going to examine what happens to carrying costs before and after tax reform.

If tax reform had no effects on interest rates, its adverse effect on carrying costs and house values would be a foregone conclusion. A $200,000 house with a $120,000 mortgage at 10 percent has interest costs of $12,000 a year before deductions and $8,640 after deductions (for someone in the 28 percent tax bracket). The monthly carrying cost is $720. Take away the deductions and the carrying cost jumps to $12,000 per year, or $1000 per month. Inevitably, the prospective purchaser faced with this change would have to settle for a cheaper house. Collectively, the reluctance of purchasers would bring house prices down so that the buyers could afford the houses on the market.

As we stressed earlier, our tax reform will immediately lower interest rates. And lower rates bring higher house prices, a point dramatically impressed on homeowners in reverse in the early 1980s, when big increases in interest severely dampened the housing market. The total effect of reform will depend on the relative strengths of the contending forces—the value of the lost interest deduction against the value of lower interest. On the one hand, we have already indicated that there are good reasons to think interest rates would fall by about 2 percentage points—say from 10 to 8 percent for mortgages. The value of the lost deduction, on the other hand, depends on just what fraction of a house a prospective purchaser intends to finance. First-time home buyers typically, but not always, finance three-quarters or more of the price of a house. Some of them have family money or other wealth and make large down payments. Families moving up by selling existing houses generally plan on much larger equity positions in their new houses. Perhaps a down payment of 50 percent is the average, so families are paying interest (and deducting) on $500 per thousand dollars of house.

A second determinant of the carrying cost is the value of the deduction set by the marginal tax rate. Among homeowners, a marginal rate of 28 percent is typical, corresponding to a taxable income of $37,000 to $89,000. Interest carrying costs per thousand dollars of house are $50 a year before taxes ($500 borrowed at 10 percent interest) and $36 a year after taxes. When tax reform comes, the interest rate will fall to 8 percent and carrying costs will be $40 a year ($500 at 8 percent) both before and after taxes. Tax reform will put this buyer behind by $4 per thousand dollars of house a year, or $800 a year for the $200,000 house.

If this $800 a year were the end of the story, it would bring a modest decline in house prices. But there is another factor we haven't touched on yet. The buyer's equity position—the down payment—must come from somewhere. By putting wealth into a house, the buyer sacrifices the return that wealth would have earned elsewhere. The alternative return from the equity in the house is another component of the carrying cost. Tax reform almost surely reduces that component. As just one example, take a couple who could put wealth into an untaxed retirement fund if they didn't put it into a house. The fund holds bonds; after reform, the interest rate on bonds would be perhaps 3 percentage points lower, and so the implicit cost of the equity would be lower by the same amount.

To take a conservative estimate, tax reform might lower the implicit cost of equity by 1 percentage point as interest rates fall. Then the carrying costs of the buyer's equity would decline by $5 ($500 at 1 percent) per thousand dollars of house a year. Recall that the buyer has come out behind by $4 on the mortgage-interest side. On net, tax reform would *lower* the carrying costs by $5 minus $4, which equals $1 per thousand, or $200 a year for the $200,000 house. Then housing prices would actually rise a tiny amount under the impetus of tax reform.

We won't argue that tax reform will stimulate the housing market. But we do feel that the potential effects on house prices are small—small enough to be lost in the ups and downs of a volatile market. Basically, reform has two effects—reducing interest rates and related costs of funds (thus stimulating housing and other asset markets) and denying interest deductions (depressing housing). To a reasonable approximation, then, these influences will cancel each other out.

If tax reform sets off a rip-roaring investment boom, interest rates might rise in the years following the immediate drop at the time of the reform. During this period, when corporations will be competing strongly with home buyers for available funds, house prices would lag behind an otherwise brisk economy. The same thing happened in the great investment boom of the late 1960s. But to get the strong economy and new jobs that go with an investment boom, minor disappointments in housing values would seem a reasonable price. In the long run, higher incomes will bring a stronger housing market.

What about the construction industry? Will a slump in new housing accompany a tax reform that banishes interest deductions, as the industry fears? The fate of the industry depends intimately on the price of existing housing. Were tax reform to depress housing by raising carrying costs, the public's interest in new houses would fall in parallel with its diminished enthusiasm for existing houses. Because tax reform will not dramatically alter carrying costs in one direction or another, it will not enrich or impoverish the construction industry.

So far, we have looked at the way prospective buyers might calculate what value of house they can afford. These calculations are the proximate determinants of house prices. But they have no bearing on the situation of an existing homeowner who has no intention of selling or buying. To the homeowner, loss of the tax deduction would be pure grief.

Our transition proposal takes care of the problem of existing mortgages without compromising the principles of the flat tax or diminishing its revenue. Homeowners would have the right to continue deducting 90 percent of their mortgage interest. Recall that the bank would then be required to pay tax on the interest it received, even though interest on new mortgages would be untaxed. Homeowners could expect to receive attractive propositions from their banks to rewrite their mortgages at an interest rate about 3 percentage points lower, but without tax deductibility. Even if banks and homeowners could not get together to lower rates, the homeowner could still deduct 90 percent of what he deducted before.

CHARITABLE CONTRIBUTIONS

Deducting contributions to worthy causes would be a thing of the past under our tax reform. Will the nation stop supporting its churches, hospitals, museums, and opera companies when the tax deduction disappears? We think not. But we should also be clear that incentives matter—the current tax system with high marginal rates and tax deductions provides inappropriately high incentives for some contributions. The immediate effect of tax reform may be a small decline in giving. Later, as the economy surges forward under the impetus of improved incentives for productive activity, giving will recover and likely exceed its current levels.

In 1991, total cash contributions to charitable causes were about $117 billion. Of this, only $61 billion was deducted on personal tax returns. Almost half of all contributions were not affected by the law permitting deduction. We confidently expect that the $56 billion in contributions being made today without any special tax benefits will continue. Further, the bulk of contributions are from people in modest tax brackets—only $28 billion in contributions were deducted in 1991 by families with taxable incomes of more than $75,000. In this connection, it is important to understand that well more than half of all cash contributions go to churches and that these gifts are generally from the middle of the income distribution.

Churches have nothing to fear from tax reform and, like most people and institutions, would have much to gain from better economic conditions brought about by reform. Despite their dominant position in gifts, churches are not the leaders in fighting a tax reform that denies deductions. Instead, institutions serving the absolute economic and social elite—universities, symphonies, opera companies, ballets, and museums—are protesting the loudest. No compelling case has ever been made that these worthy undertakings should be financed by anyone but their customers. A glance at the crowd in any of them will tell you that it is perverse to tax the typical American to subsidize the elite institutions. But granting tax deductions for gifts is precisely such a subsidy.

Tax reform will be a tremendous boon to the economic elite from the start. After all, those with high salaries will benefit directly and immediately from the reduction in the tax rate from 39.6 percent to 19 percent. Those with lightly taxed business income stand to benefit more indirectly in that their economic activities are severely distorted by the devices and activities they have adopted to avoid taxes. Freed from these distortions, they may well become better off even though they are paying more taxes. For both groups, removing tax deductions from their favorite cultural activities is a reasonable price to pay. With substantially higher after-tax incomes among their customers as well as donors, universities and other institutions will make up part or perhaps all of the ground they will lose when tax deductions disappear.

Major tax cuts in 1981 and 1986 cut the top marginal tax rate from 70 percent to 50 percent and then to 28 percent. As a result, major donors shifted from spending thirty-three-cent dollars to spending fifty-cent and then seventy-two-cent dollars for tax-deductible gifts. Despite these major reductions in incentives for the rich to give, donations to charity grew robustly (see table 4.2). Thus, there is a sound basis for our projection that contributions will not decline when the tax incentive diminishes.

THE FEDERAL DEFICIT

The federal deficit is one of the most conspicuous problems of the American economy. In 1993, the government spent about $255 billion more than it took in. The same thing seems likely to happen in future years. Is the federal government headed for bankruptcy? Is it essential to raise additional revenue in the near future in order to close the deficit? Would the flat tax be a better vehicle for raising the needed revenue?

Barring a miracle, the federal government will continue to operate seriously in the red for the rest of the 1990s. Experience in the past two decades shows that the federal government inevitably runs a deficit. Should the deficit threaten to shrink, politicians will rush in with tax cuts and spending increases to push the deficit

Table 4.2   Total Charitable Contributions
versus Amount Deducted

Year	Total Gifts (billions of dollars)	Tax Deductions (billions of dollars)
1979	$43	$24
1980	49	26
1981	55	31
1982	59	33
1983	63	38
1984	69	42
1985	73	48
1986	84	54
1987	90	50
1988	98	51
1989	107	55
1990	112	57
1991	117	61
1992	122	Not available
1993	126	Not available

back to its normal high level. Because both tax rates and spending respond to the economic and political environment, no change in the tax system could make a permanent change in the deficit. Still, there are two ways that the flat tax would alter the environment. First, the flat tax will lower interest rates. Under our transition proposal, the government's outstanding debt would benefit immediately from the lower interest rates that would automatically accompany a reform that put interest on an after-tax basis. Second, the flat tax will stimulate economic growth. Because growth raises revenue more quickly than spending, it will further help reduce the deficit or permit lower taxes or higher spending.

If we are right that a chronic deficit is the inevitable result of political equilibrium, the effect of higher tax rates under either the current tax or the flat tax is more spending, not a lower deficit. Only a constitutional change in the taxing and spending system could alter the political equilibrium, not a switch to the flat tax.

LIFE IN A 19 PERCENT WORLD

What would life be like in a world with a 19 percent flat tax? The most important change is that we would spend time thinking about producing goods and services and improving productivity instead of remaining obsessed with exploiting tax-advantaged opportunities. With 40 percent top marginal rates, many high-income people feel that they cannot afford to reveal *any* significant income to the IRS. They put great effort into reducing taxable income and diverting their incomes to tax-free destinations. At 40 cents on the dollar, dishonesty is lucrative. At 19 percent, most people would relax. Evasion and avoidance are far less profitable at 19 percent than at 40 percent. Conversely, keeping eighty-one cents of every additional dollar of income is a stimulus to produce as much as possible. With taxes taking no more than nineteen cents from each additional dollar at every income level, most people will pursue those economic activities that bring the highest return and the most satisfaction, rather than the ones that minimize taxable income.

Think of the everyday kinds of decisions most people make that are governed by a steeply graduated tax-rate structure. Tickets for box seats at baseball stadiums, club memberships, business travel, company cars, and a host of other business outlays that incorporated and un-incorporated firms regularly purchase would now cost the owners of that business eighty-one cents of after-tax income, rather than the current sixty cents. Business would be expected to run a tighter ship with the much higher returns that a 19 percent rate affords over current high rates.

Those who believe that life would grind to a halt with the loss of deductions for interest and charitable contributions need to consider how they would alter their lives the morning the flat tax took effect. They would fire their lawyers and accountants and instead seek advice and information on sound economic investments. Perhaps most important for the ordinary working American, the 19 percent world would abolish the annual nightmare of tax-return preparation in April. Both Forms 1 and 2 could be filled out in a few minutes on the basis of records that everyone keeps anyway.

5. Questions and Answers about the Flat Tax

WE HAVE PRESENTED the flat tax and answered questions about it on radio talk shows, before professional and lay audiences, before congressional committees, and in interviews with newspaper and magazine reporters. In this chapter we have assembled the most asked questions together with our answers, a format we hope will answer any questions you may have about the flat tax.

DEDUCTIONS

Q: *What about charitable deductions?*

A: No charitable deductions would be allowed under the flat tax. We do not believe that current tax incentives are a major part of why people, apart from the very rich, contribute to community, religious, and other organizations. Almost half of all contributions are made by people who take the standard deduction and thus do not benefit from an itemized deduction for charitable contributions. However, the tax code allows deductible gifts of appreciated property, such as stock or works of art, thus allowing wealthy taxpayers to pay little or no taxes. On net, you, the average taxpayer, will save more by blocking the tax-avoiding tricks of the wealthy than you will lose from eliminating tax deductions from your own contributions. Remember, the value of any deduction depends on your tax bracket: if you are in the 15 percent bracket, you get less than one-third the benefit of someone who is in the 39.6 percent bracket. There is little merit in public subsidy for organizations whose success in raising funds depends on tax deductibility rather than the intrinsic merits of their activities.

Q: *But aren't there many deserving activities that will disappear if charitable contributions are no longer deductible?*

A: The simple answer is no. Remember, the top rate fell from 70 percent in 1980 to 28 percent in 1986, until it was increased to 31 percent beginning with the 1991 tax year. During 1980—1989, individual giving grew at a compound annual rate of 5.2 percent despite the fact that the benefit of deducting contributions declined from a maximum refund of seventy cents on the dollar to no more than twenty-eight cents. Compared with the 1980s, individual giving grew at a much slower compound annual rate of 3.1 percent between 1955 and 1980, a period of much higher marginal rates. In real terms, expressed in constant (inflation-adjusted) 1990 dollars, individual giving increased from $64.7 billion in 1980 to $102 billion in 1989. Sustained, strong economic growth, which increased the real income of the average American, was the most important factor in the sharp rise in giving, far more important than any tax break. Indeed, the real 57.7 percent increase in total individual giving in the 1980s greatly exceeded the 32.8 percent growth in real total consumer expenditures. The 1980s, a period of steadily declining tax rates, was more a period of giving than of greed.

Q: *What would happen to the restaurant industry?*

A: Business meals in restaurants would be fully deductible as business expenses under the flat tax, an improvement over the current situation, where only 50 percent of meals are deductible. Lower tax rates, in contrast, would reduce the incentive for businesses to splurge on restaurant meals. The net effect on the restaurant industry would probably be around zero.

Q: *Shouldn't the tax system provide some relief to families with high medical costs?*

A: Virtually the entire U.S. population is now covered by medical insurance, Medicare, or medical benefits through welfare. The medical deduction under the current personal income tax is a source of many abuses, including the deduction of swimming pools and other home improvements that are available only to the wealthy. Remember, the higher the marginal rate, the greater the tax benefit of any deduction. The nearly half of all taxpayers who take the standard deduction, the bottom half of the income distribution, rarely take advantage of this deduction. Few families would suffer, and the overwhelming majority would gain by closing off this source of abuse.

The IRS publication Statistics of Income reported that only 5.5 million of the 113.8 million returns filed in 1992 selected medical and dental expense deductions, with a total value of $25.5 billion. The richest 5 percent of those 5.5 million returns took more than 10 percent of total medical deductions, which means the richer you are, the greater the tax subsidy you receive—which is surely absurd.

Q: *What about alimony?*

A: Under the flat tax, the spouse that pays alimony does not get to deduct it and therefore pays the tax on it. The spouse that receives it does not pay any additional taxes. This is as fair as the current arrangement but eliminates the opportunity to take advantage of differences between the tax rates of the two sexes.

Q: *Why is there no deduction for moving costs in the flat tax?*

A: Moving costs are only one of hundreds of costs incurred by taxpayers in order to earn an income. It is inconsistent to permit deduction of moving costs when costs of commuting, purchase of special clothing, and other employment costs cannot be deducted. Many moves are undertaken for reasons unrelated to earning a higher income and so should not escape taxation. The deduction for moving expenses is one of a number of tax provisions abused by a small minority of taxpayers at the expense of the great majority. It should be eliminated. Eliminating each tax break enlarges the tax base, which permits lower rates to generate sufficient revenue to run the government.

Q: *I am a salaried employee. How would I treat unreimbursed business expenses? There is no room for this deduction on the simple individual wage tax form.*

A: Deducting so-called business expenses of salaried employees is a major loophole in the current tax system in that it subsidizes summer travel for teachers, trips to conventions, and other activities for which special incentives are inappropriate. Genuine business expenses ought to be borne by employers, in which case they are deductible under the business tax.

Q: *Won't state and local governments be irrevocably damaged in their capacity to tax local residents if the federal deduction for state and local taxes is eliminated?*

A: Who benefits from this deduction? Primarily wealthy taxpayers. Altogether, slightly fewer than 32 million returns, about 28 percent of those filed in 1992, claimed this deduction. Among these, the richest 22 percent of taxpayers, those with adjusted gross incomes over $75,000, got the benefit of half the $159 billion claimed in deductions. Recalculated, just over 6 percent of all taxpayers claimed

$80 billion, about half, of all itemized deductions for state and local taxes. This deduction amounts to a huge benefit for the richest Americans and for those states in which the rich disproportionately live, such as New York, Connecticut, and California, at the expense of North Dakota, Alabama, and Tennessee.

Moreover, current law is less generous than it was a decade ago. Sales taxes, which were deductible as recently as 1986, are no longer deductible. State and local governments did not collapse when this deduction was removed from the federal income tax. Moreover, itemized deductions can no longer be deducted in full above adjusted gross income of $108,450 (married, filing jointly). Form 1040 includes a ten-line worksheet in which you are asked to calculate and subtract "excess itemized deductions." The worksheet invites you to multiply 80 percent of most of your itemized deductions, subtract $108,450 (married, filing jointly), multiply the difference by 3 percent, enter the smaller of line 4 or line 8, subtract that sum from total itemized deductions, and enter the balance on Schedule A. Because Congress has an insatiable appetite for more revenue, we expect it to further limit the itemized deduction for state and local taxes, if not eliminate it altogether. Under the flat tax, those who lose this benefit gain from the incentive of lower rates.

Q: *What about interest deductions?*

A: The flat tax would end the deduction for interest of

all kinds. (See the next Q & A for the answer to home mortgage interest in particular.) As recently as 1986, credit card and charge account interest were deductible. In 1987, only 65 percent of personal interest was deductible. In 1993, only home mortgage interest was deductible, up to a maximum of $1 million. In 1992, less than 0.1 percent of all returns could exploit this maximum. Altogether, 14 million filers (12 percent of all returns) with adjusted gross incomes of more than $50,000 claimed 68 percent of all interest deductions. About 88 percent of all taxpayers get no or little benefit. Remember, the higher your tax bracket, the greater your tax benefit. The number of nondeductible interest items listed in Form 1040 has steadily expanded in recent years.

The flat tax changes the tax treatment of interest for businesses and individuals. All interest is placed on an after-tax basis. Interest expense is no longer deductible by business, and interest income is no longer taxable to individuals. The level of interest rates in the economy will fall from the high level of taxable corporate bonds to the low level of tax-free municipal bonds. Taxpayers who lose interest deductions will benefit from lower interest rates overall.

HOUSING

Q: *What would happen to the housing market as a result of ending the deduction for mortgage interest?*

A: The flat tax eliminates the deduction for all kinds of interest, not just mortgage interest. It would not discriminate against housing. However, improvements in the taxation of business investment would tend to draw wealth out of housing and into plant, equipment, and other business investment, which might reduce housing values temporarily. The effect would not be more than a few percent and would last only for the duration of the investment boom set off by the new tax system. In the longer run, the outlook for housing values would be improved as overall economic activity increased in response to the tax.

Q: *The only way I can afford my house today is the large tax deduction I get for the interest on my mortgage. Won't I have to sell my house if I can no longer take the deduction?*

A: The parallel removal of interest deduction and interest taxation under the flat tax will bring about lower interest rates. Lower interest rates reduce monthly mortgage payments, which offsets the loss of mortgage interest deduction for most taxpayers. Only the wealthiest taxpayers may lose out from the elimination of mortgage interest, but they receive compensation in the form of lower rates. A transition measure would allow present homeowners to deduct 90 percent of their interest until they renegotiated the loans at the new, lower rate.

Q: *Why shouldn't we tax the capital gains from the sale of a house?*

A: These capital gains are rarely taxed under the current system because of the rollover provision, forgiveness of $125,000 of capital gains for those aged fifty-five and over, and the stepping up of the basis for capital gains at the time of inheritance. We believe that taxing housing is properly ceded to local governments under our federal system. Local property taxes capture part of the value of the services of a house.

Q: *I own a building that is part of a low-income housing project, for which I get a low-income housing credit. If you take this credit away from me, what will happen to those poor people who live in low-income housing projects?*

A: Like all the credits in the existing tax system, such as the jobs credit for business employers who hire members of special targeted groups, credit for alcohol used as fuel, credit for increasing research activities, disabled access credit, enhanced oil recovery credit, renewable electricity production credit, and qualified electric vehicle credit, the low-income housing credit would disappear with the advent of the flat tax. All these credits distort the economy and narrow the tax base, thereby raising rates for everybody else. These tax credits result in taxpayers' money being put into elaborate installations and activities that are at or below the margin of economic efficiency. It would be far more efficient for the government to subsidize these activities directly, rather than indirectly through the tax code.

In particular, poor people need not suffer; the government could give them cash or housing vouchers to find housing in the market economy.

The tax system is not the proper place to undertake social engineering. The merits and financing of social programs are subjects for open public discussion during the annual appropriations process in which members of Congress have to vote on the record for each expenditure. These programs should not be tucked away in the tax system. Our present complicated, costly income tax is partly the result of using the tax system for social engineering, instead of simply to collect revenue.

Q: *Because your plan removes the tax incentives now offered for preserving historic structures, won't this accelerate the destruction of many buildings that belong to our national heritage and that should be saved for future generations to enjoy?*

A: For every genuinely important historic building saved by the tax incentives, dozens or perhaps even hundreds of buildings are subsidized that are not important or would be kept by their owners anyway. Giving tax incentives for historic structures is a terribly inefficient way to accomplish the goal of preservation—most of its effect is to create another tax shelter. Directly appropriating government funds for saving individual buildings is a far superior social policy for preservation.

Q: *Doesn't the flat tax encourage speculation in land by granting first-year write-off for land purchases?*

A: The sellers of land have to count their proceeds as taxable income; this offsets the deduction granted to the purchaser. Prices of undeveloped residential land may rise a little, but with a 19 percent tax rate, the effect should be small. Land transactions are included in the flat tax because it is difficult to separate the value of land from the value of the buildings on it.

INTERGOVERNMENTAL RELATIONS

Q: *How would local governments be affected by the change in the taxation of bonds?*

A: Local governments derive a small advantage from the tax-free status of their bonds and the taxation of all competing bonds in the current system. Able to borrow at artificially low rates, state and local governments have issued billions of dollars in debt that is unwarranted for legitimate public purposes. Many bond issues finance questionable activities, as is evidenced by state legislators' refusing to vote for higher taxes. Excess state and local borrowing also diverts money away from more productive corporate uses.

Under the flat tax, local government bonds would remain untaxed, but all other bonds would also provide tax-free interest because the earnings of business would be taxed at the source. Corporate bonds would be placed on a level playing field with government bonds. The immediate impact would lower the borrowing costs of other borrowers to the levels paid by local governments. In the ensuing investment boom, as interest rates rise, local borrowing costs would gradually rise. The slightly adverse effect on local governments would be confined to a few years and would not be large. In the longer run, local governments would face no higher interest rates and would benefit in many other ways from the improved performance of the U.S. economy. There is simply no substitute for a prosperous citizenry.

Q: *What about such other taxes as state, county, excise, and sales taxes? What would happen to them under the flat tax?*

A: Although we would prefer that other units of government besides the federal government switch to taxes based on the same principle as the flat tax, we have limited our proposal to federal action. The only important implication of our proposal for other federal taxes is the elimination of the deduction for state and local income taxes and property taxes under the federal income tax (the deduction for state and local sales taxes was eliminated in 1987). This deduction overwhelmingly favors rich people; just over 6 percent of all taxpayers, those with adjusted gross incomes over $75,000, get half the benefit. But these same taxpayers benefit from lower rates under the flat tax. Remember, every time a deduction is eliminated, the tax base is broadened. The broader the base, the lower the tax rate. Eliminating this deduction also promotes efficiency by reducing the incentive to channel economic activity through state and local governments to exploit a tax break.

Q: *How does the flat tax affect state income taxes where the tax returns are linked to the federal tax system?*

A: Because the flat tax would raise approximately the same revenue as the old tax system, a state that retained the linkage would continue to receive about the same revenue as well.

Q: *How does the flat tax treat government? Are state and local activities taxed? Does the federal government tax itself?*

A: State and local governments pay no taxes themselves, but their employees pay the individual wage tax. The same is true for the federal government.

THE INDIVIDUAL WAGE TAX

Q: *The current income tax does not tax fringe benefits. Your flat tax doesn't tax them either, but it also doesn't permit my employer to deduct them. What will happen to my fringe benefits under the simple tax?*

A: Fringe benefits arose in World War II as employers tried to find a way to pay their employees more under stringent wartime regulations. During the past fifty years, employees have often struggled harder for better fringe benefits than for pay increases because of the tax-free status of fringes. Today, fringe benefits are an extremely important part of any compensation package, and your employer will not cut your benefits without compensating you in some other way.

Fringe benefits are among the largest contributors to narrowing the tax base. It is important to include the value of fringe benefits in the tax base; otherwise, tax rates, levied on a smaller tax base, will remain unnecessarily high. The flat tax eliminates the distortion toward fringe benefits created by the fact that employers can deduct them, thereby receiving a subsidy that can be passed on to their employees. The best alternative, and one we expect your employer to select, is to offer you higher pay in exchange for lower fringes. You can then use the extra cash to buy whatever combination of benefits you desire or for any other purpose, such as travel, housing, educational expenses, and so forth.

Q: *My teenage daughter has taken a part-time job and will earn about $3,000 this year. Can she use the personal allowance of $9,500 to avoid paying tax? Will I lose my dependent's allowance of $4,500 for her?*

A: All taxpayers are entitled to the personal allowance, including your daughter. You will retain the dependent's allowance as long as you provide more than half her total support over the year.

Q: *I am an American citizen and now enjoy a $70,000 exclusion for income earned abroad. How will this income be treated under the flat tax?*

A: All income earned from work performed abroad, or from enterprises located abroad, will be taxed by the country where you earn it. The flat tax applies only to the domestic operations of all businesses, regardless of ownership. The flat tax would not apply to the foreign earnings of Americans.

Q: *The flat tax eliminates the credit for child and dependent care expenses. Won't this force people to stay home to take care of their children and elderly dependents, thereby increasing their dependence on welfare, reducing their participation in the labor force, and costing the government more money than it would save from its elimination?*

A: Like many of the complicated, special provisions in the tax system, the child care credit fails to focus its benefits in an area of particular social need. It potentially lowers the taxes of a significant fraction of all taxpayers—families with two earners and one or more children. It is available at all income levels. In 1993, for example, even the very rich were able to claim a credit of $480, although some taxpayers subject to the alternative minimum tax were not eligible for the full credit. Higher tax rates are required to compensate for this lowering of the amount of taxes. Features like the child care credit are antithetical to the flat-tax philosophy, which favors the broadest possible tax base with the lowest tax rate. We think that the special problems of helping families with child care and other responsibilities should be attacked specifically within the welfare system, not with the scattergun of the tax system. The flat tax provides plenty of revenue for a generous welfare program.

Q: *Isn't it unfair to start taxing workers' compensation benefits and insurance for injury or sickness?*

A: Workers' compensation benefits are money that replaces wages when a worker is disabled on the job. The wages themselves would have been taxed, so it stands to reason that the replacement should be taxed. Failure to tax workers' compensation benefits creates an inappropriate incentive for workers to remain off the job after a period of disability.

Q: *Why does the flat tax eliminate the extra exemptions for the blind and the elderly? What makes you want to lay higher taxes on these two especially unfortunate groups in our society?*

A: Many of the elderly and a few of the blind are well off. It raises everybody's tax rate inappropriately to provide extra exemptions to every elderly and blind individual. The road to a narrowly based, high-rate tax system begins with just a few small loopholes. It is far better, and more conducive to both an efficient economy and a simple tax system, to use Social Security and other social programs, which supply the lion's share of the incomes of many elderly persons, and other public or private welfare organizations to assist the blind.

Q: *Part of my compensation comes in the form of stock options. How are these taxed?*

A: The full market value of the options is included in your compensation in the year you receive them, whether or not you exercise them.

THE BUSINESS TAX

Q: *What would happen to the unused depreciation deductions from capital investments made under the old tax system?*

A: It is important to keep in mind that this is a not an issue of tax policy but of how to make the transition from the complicated, costly current code to the simple, efficient flat tax. The first point to note is that much lower tax rates make these deductions much less important. From the standpoint of the economy as a whole, the reduced taxation of the earnings of capital under the flat tax offsets the decline in the value of the deductions because of lower tax rates. From the point of view of each business, a first-year write-off is more attractive than multiyear depreciation deductions for all new investment.

However, some firms may not be planning to make new investments in the immediate future, but would lose out if their scheduled depreciation deductions were taken away. How much money is at stake? In 1992, total depreciation deductions under the personal and corporate taxes came to $597 billion. At the 35 percent corporate rate, and at a similar average rate for individual recipients of most business income, those deductions were worth $209 billion. If Congress chooses to honor unused depreciation predating tax reform, it would take $597 billion out of the tax base for 1995. This would require an increase in the tax rate from 19 percent to 20.1 percent. But, this slightly higher tax rate would only be temporary, to last no more than five years, as the transition depreciation is paid off. The rate would then be reset at 19 percent.

An alternative approach, which would not require a temporary increase in the tax rate, would let firms choose to take the depreciation deductions but would limit their write-off of new investment to, say, half the purchase price of new investment. They could take the remaining half as soon as they chose not to continue to take the old depreciation. Each firm could select the most advantageous strategy.

Q: *I'm a traveling saleswoman. I earn commissions and pay my own travel expenses. I do not receive a salary. How would I fill out the flat tax?*

A: All self-employed individuals will file Form 2, the business tax form, where they can deduct travel and other business expenses. To take advantage of the personal allowance, you will want to pay yourself a salary of at least $16,500 if you are married. Report this amount along with your husband's earnings on Form 1, the individual wage tax. In this way you will be able to deduct your legitimate business expenses and receive the personal allowance. You will need to keep records to document your income and expenses.

Q: *You say that the current system taxes income twice. Isn't income income no matter what its source?*

A: Income is an individual's command over resources. Only people have income. The income of a corporation is just the income of its owners, the stockholders. The current system taxes the same income twice, once when the corporation receives it and again when it is paid as dividends to stockholders. The combined tax rate on this single stream of income, 34 percent on the corporation and up to 39.6 percent on dividends received by individuals, is 60 percent. This does not take into account additional state taxes. Double taxation amounts to confiscation, which violates every concept and definition of fair.

Q: *What about capital gains? You eliminate the taxation of capital gains on the sale of financial assets, claiming that it also amounts to double taxation. Won't the elimination of capital gains give a windfall to business and the rich?*

A: First, capital gains are taxed under the flat tax. Capital gains from the sale of business property—an office or apartment building or a house held for investment purposes—would be taxed under the business tax, which treats the proceeds from the sale of plant, equipment, and buildings as taxable income for the business. Capital gains on stocks, bonds, and other financial instruments are a separate matter; they arise from the capitalization of after-tax income. As the earnings of a business grow, the value of a share of stock also rises because stock constitutes a claim on the firm's after-tax income. Remember, all business earnings are fully taxed at 19 percent. Another tax on the appreciation of shares would amount to a second tax on a single stream of income. Put another way, share values rise because investors have every reason to believe that retained earnings, which permit firms to expand, significantly increase the probability of higher future earnings.

As to residential property, capital gains on owner-occupied homes arise from the capitalization of rental values, which are heavily taxed by state and local governments; again, it would be double taxation for the federal government to tax the capital gains as well. Finally, it must be recognized that a good part of any capital gains on owner-occupied homes is simply inflation, especially for those who have remained in their homes a long time. If an effective, comprehensive capital gains tax were imposed on owner-occupied homes under current law, many homeowners would actually pay a tax on their original purchase price, a confiscation of capital, because the tax code does not provide for indexing the buying and selling prices of any asset for inflation.

Q: *How are tax losses for individuals and businesses treated?*

A: Remember that self-employed persons fill out the business tax form just as a large corporation does. Business losses can be carried forward without limit to offset future profits (assuming your bank or rich relatives will keep lending you money). There is no such thing as a tax loss under the individual wage tax. You can't reduce your compensation tax by generating business losses. Well-paid individuals who farm as a hobby or engage in other dubious sidelines to shelter their wages from the IRS had better enjoy their costly hobbies; the IRS will not give them any break under the flat tax.

Q: *Would a company going bankrupt get a tax refund in proportion to its loss?*

A: No. The flat tax would never make payments (except refunds of overpayments) to taxpayers. However, a bankrupt company could be acquired by another firm, which would assume the tax loss.

Q: *Some companies pay so much interest today that disallowing the deduction of interest would make them operate at a loss. Isn't this bad economic policy?*

A: This is a problem only during the transition to the flat tax. Corporations and homeowners with large amounts of debt will suffer, just as those with large holdings of bonds or mortgages will gain. For two reasons, the problem is not serious. First, the dramatic reduction in the tax rate to 19 percent largely offsets the increase in taxes from the loss of interest deductions in most cases. Second, most corporate debt can be called and reissued at lower rates when the flat tax is law. As for homeowners, incentives can be provided to encourage banks and other lending institutions to rewrite home mortgages at the new, lower interest rates that will prevail when the flat tax is put into place.

Q: *If a firm plowed back all its income into plant and equipment, and hence paid no business tax, couldn't the firm increase its value forever without paying taxes? Wouldn't the stockholders receive the capitalized value of the firm as untaxed capital gains?*

A: Sooner or later, the firm will run out of sufficiently profitable opportunities and will start paying out its income to its owners instead of plowing it back. If the market didn't believe this, the stock would have no value because the stockholders would not believe that they were ever going to get anything; stockholders would sell their shares to buy stock in firms that were paying out some of their income to their owners. The market will always know that the tax will be imposed on any returns earned by the stockholders, so the market value of the firm will always be the capitalized value after taxes.

Q: *Won't businesses constantly buy and sell equipment or land in order to take advantage of the immediate write-off?*

A: No. There is nothing to be gained from extra purchases and sales. The proceeds of the sale of any equipment must be reported as income to be taxed, which offsets the tax benefits of a subsequent purchase. The only winner is the broker who executes the sale.

Q: *How are individuals taxed on their rental activities? Is rental income part of wages or business income? Would individuals have to file both business and individual tax forms if they had both kinds of income?*

A: Renting is definitely a business activity and would require a business tax form. Rental receipts are taxed as business income, but purchase of rental property qualifies for a first-year write-off. Because there are no complicated depreciation computations, little effort would be required to fill out the business tax form for rental units. If rental income is your only source of income, you should pay yourself a salary from rental income and fill out the wage form to take advantage of the generous personal allowance enjoyed by every taxpayer.

Q: *If my company provides me with subsidized lunches, physical exercise facilities, a company car, and other benefits, how are these treated under the flat tax?*

A: Your company cannot deduct fringe benefits under the business tax. It can only deduct cash payments paid out as wages and salaries. It can still provide you with fringe benefits, but these no longer enjoy any tax benefits; you would be better off taking the value of fringe benefits in cash and spending the money any way you want, buying only those services you truly require.

Q: *I am involved in a highly leveraged investment company. Won't my company and others like it be forced out of business because we will no longer be able to deduct interest expenses?*

A: It is true that you will no longer be able to deduct interest expenses. But it is likely that your borrowing is linked to market interest rates. Remember, the decline in interest rates caused by the flat tax will offset most or all the loss of the deduction. Also, don't forget that the income from your company will be taxed at only 19 percent. Try filling out the business tax form to see what will happen to your total tax payment.

Q: *Does the flat tax cover the fringe benefits of government and nonprofit organizations?*

A: Yes. They are required to file the business form in a particular way that exempts all their income except what is paid to their employees as fringe benefits. In this way, the flat tax avoids a distortion in favor of government and nonprofit activities that would arise if they alone could pay untaxed fringes.

Q: *How will the flat tax affect the value of the U.S. dollar in the foreign exchange markets?*

A: The tax treatment of imports and exports of goods and services will be essentially the same under the flat tax as under the existing system, so there will be no change in the value of the dollar on that account. The lower interest rates that will accompany the adoption of the flat tax may bring a temporary decline in the value of the dollar, which will stimulate U.S. exports and discourage imports, but this will be a one-time adjustment only.

Q: *Will foreign investment in the United States increase or decrease under the flat tax?*

A: The flat tax is 19 percent for business firms and individuals. In addition, business firms can use 100 percent first-year write-off of new investment, and individuals do not pay capital gains taxes. The flat tax makes the business climate in the United States far more attractive than that in every country in Western Europe and most other countries. Foreign investment should pour into the United States after the flat tax is adopted. The inflow of foreign investment will raise the value of the U.S. dollar in foreign exchange markets.

Q: *Why does the flat tax collect the business tax from firms and the wage tax from individuals? Wouldn't it be easier and simpler to just use one form and collect both taxes from firms or from individuals?*

A: The IRS has not been terribly successful in trying to collect income taxes on interest and dividends from individuals. A distinct advantage of the flat tax is that it permits airtight collection of taxes on business income at the source, where enforcement is easiest. Remember, the low 19 percent rate significantly reduces the benefits of cheating, which will help ensure fuller reporting of all business income.

We make individuals fill out the wage tax for two main reasons. First, it ensures that taxpayers get the benefits of their personal allowance. The tax-withholding system already in place can be adapted to collect almost exactly the full amount of taxes each individual owes, so that taxpayers would not be faced with a large bill at the end of the year. This is relatively easy to do with a 19 percent flat tax.

Second, it is crucial that all taxpayers do an annual accounting of their taxes every year to determine how much they are paying for government services. The beauty of the flat tax is that all taxpayers would pay higher taxes in the same proportion to pay for new government programs. If individuals did not file returns, advocates of more government spending could promise voters new benefits without higher costs. They would promise to place new taxes solely on rich, anonymous corporations, as if those taxes will not affect the employees or the owners of those corporations. Remember, businesses don't pay taxes; only individuals do. And higher taxes on business are borne in part by the employees in the form of fewer jobs and lower wages.

TAX REFORM AND THE RICH

Q: *You keep talking about broadening the tax base. What's so important about this?*

A: Tax rates are high today because the tax base is so narrow. Personal income in the United States is about $5 trillion. A raft of exclusions reduces this number to about $3.6 trillion in adjusted gross income and $2.4 trillion in taxable income. A lower rate on all or most personal income would collect the same amount of money as a much higher rate on taxable income.

The same situation applies to business income. Much of this income escapes taxation because it does not fall into the net of taxable income. Altogether, less than half the national income is subject to income taxation, which means that relatively high rates of tax are required to collect enough money to run the government. The only way to enjoy the economic benefits of low tax rates and achieve real simplification is to broaden the tax base to all national income. The only exclusions in the flat-tax base from the entire gross domestic product are personal allowances, which inject a large measure of progressivity into the flat tax, and the investment incentive of 100 percent first-year write-off, which transforms the flat tax into a tax on consumption.

Q: *What's so important about choosing a 19 percent rate? Why not 18 percent or 20 percent?*

A: Actually, 19 percent is not, in and of itself, critical. It is important that the rate be low, so 18 percent or 20 percent would be acceptable. When we first designed our integrated, simple flat-tax proposal in 1981, we calculated that 19 percent would be revenue neutral, which means that it would collect the same amount of money in 1981 as the then personal and corporate income taxes. We have stayed with

19 percent partly out of loyalty to our original plan and to retain name recognition for it. But we have also stuck with 19 percent to avoid breaking through what is for us a politically important psychological barrier of 20 percent. We do not want politicians to add fractions or whole percentage points to the tax rate that would rapidly push rates up into the mid or high 20s.

Q: *Personal and corporate income taxes generate revenues that equal about 11 percent of the gross domestic product. So why can't you use a flat rate of 11 percent?*

A: We could. However, an 11 percent flat tax would not permit the inclusion of a large personal allowance that exempts poor people from income taxes or include any provision for depreciation. Personal allowances amount to about 27 percent of GDP, and our 100 percent first-year write-off amounts to about another 11 percent. When this 38 percent of GDP is subtracted from the tax base, a rate of 19 percent is required to generate the same revenues as the current income tax.

It is possible, of course, to have smaller personal allowances and stretched-out depreciation, which would permit a lower flat rate of tax. But that mix would impose higher taxes on low-income households and provide less in the way of investment incentives. We believe that our package—100 percent first-year write-off, large personal allowances, and a 19 percent rate—is the best mix.

Q: *Isn't the flat tax a windfall to the rich?*

A: Taxation of families with high incomes and few deductions would be dramatically reduced under the flat tax. But those who have taken advantage of the many opportunities in the tax code to reduce or postpone taxes through tax shelters, large deductions, purchasing municipal bonds, and other gimmicks will pay significantly higher taxes. Those who work hard will do better; those who have concentrated on avoiding tax will do worse.

Remember, the flat tax includes a generous personal allowance. This means that millions of working families will no longer pay any income taxes. Those in the middle class will face a lower rate of tax. The flat tax will improve every taxpayer's incentive to work, save, and invest and shift from avoiding or reducing taxes to producing income.

Q: *Won't the flat tax be a step backward in terms of fairness? Isn't it less progressive than the current income tax?*

A: In our view, the flat tax, under which every taxpayer pays the same rate and no taxpayer is exempt from taxation, is much fairer than the current income tax with its unfathomable complexity and unconscionably high compliance costs. Remember, until recently, fairness meant equal treatment under the law. Equating fairness and making the rich pay more is a modern invention of those who believe the tax system should be used to redistribute income to make everyone equal.

The good news is that the flat tax is progressive in that families with higher incomes pay a larger fraction of their income in taxes. Families with incomes below the personal allowance level pay no tax at all. For a married couple, filing jointly, with two children, there is no tax on the first $25,500 of income. The proportion of income paid in tax rises to close to 19 percent for the highest income. For 1995, the proportions of income paid as tax for this four-person family are

Income	Tax
$10,000	0.0%
$20,000	0.0%
$30,000	2.9%
$40,000	6.9%
$50,000	9.3%
$75,000	12.6%
$100,000	14.2%
$200,000	16.6%

Finally, recall the history of reductions in tax rates in the 1920s, 1960s, and 1980s. In every case, the share of taxes paid by the rich increased while the share of taxes paid by lower- and middle-income categories fell. Since the 1990 tax increase went into effect, the share of taxes paid by the richest few percent has declined, while the share paid by the poor and middle classes has increased. Higher tax rates achieve the opposite effect of their proponents' intentions.

Q: *Will business pay its fair share of taxes under the flat tax?*

A: It must be repeated over and over again that only people pay taxes. Remember, the true incidence or burden of income taxes on corporations is not fully known—some is effectively paid by owners, some by employees, and some by consumers (who are workers in another guise). The flat tax is designed to collect all the tax that business owes, much of which escapes taxation under the current system because the IRS attempts to collect it from individuals instead of at the source.

Income from business sources is taxed at the same rate as income from employment, so that all productive economic activity is taxed fairly—at the same rate. Under the current system, some business income is taxed at excessive rates because of the double taxation of corporate dividends and capital gains. Other business income is lightly taxed or even subsidized through tax shelters, such as farming income.

Q: *Isn't the flat tax unfair because rich people can live off interest and capital gains income and thereby pay no taxes?*

A: The flat tax puts the equivalent of a withholding tax on interest and capital gains. The business tax applies to business income before it is paid out as interest or if it is retained in the business and generates capital gains for stockholders. The interest, dividends, and capital gains received by individuals in all income categories have already been taxed under the business tax. The rich, along with all other recipients of business income, have already been taxed under the business tax—they cannot escape it. What they receive as dividends, interest, or capital gains is after-tax income, in exactly the same way that recipients of wages receive take-home pay.

Q: *Won't part of the tax on capital (on business) be shifted onto consumers in the form of higher prices rather than being paid by the owners of the capital? Isn't this unequal treatment relative to the wage tax, which cannot be shifted?*

A: Yes. There is a fundamental difference between capital, which is a produced input, and labor, which is a primary, unproduced input to the economy. Because the flat tax permits first-year write-off of investment, it puts no tax on the marginal addition to capital. The tax benefit of the write-off in the first year counterbalances the taxes that will be paid from its productivity in the future—the 19 percent deduction for investment write-off equals the 19 percent tax on future higher earnings.

Higher rates of economic growth mean higher incomes, higher wages, and higher living standards for all Americans. The growth in revenue from the flat tax comes primarily from growth in the number of and real incomes of paid employees because value added by labor represents three-quarters of the gross domestic product. Recipients of capital income will also pay more in taxes as the stock of capital expands in the country.

A last comment: Economists of all persuasions agree that a tax on consumption rather than income would increase efficiency; some argue that it might increase the growth rate. The flat tax converts the income tax into a tax on consumption as it exempts all new investment from the tax base each year. It does, however, tax the returns to that investment in future years as it shows up in higher productivity and output.

NONPROFIT ORGANIZATIONS

Q: *How does the simple tax treat nonprofit organizations?*

A: They are exempt from the business tax, but their employees must pay the individual wage tax. As under present law, their dividends are untaxed. Nonprofit organizations cannot benefit from the investment incentive of first-year write-off.

Q: *What about nonbusiness entities such as trusts, estates, or charitable organizations, including churches and schools?*

A: Any actual business owned by one of these entities must file the business tax form. Their employees must pay the individual wage tax. Otherwise, these entities are not taxed. Note that a conventional personal trust, which holds stock and bonds, deals en-

tirely in after-tax income, so there is no reason for
the tax system to pay attention to it.

INHERITANCE

Q: *What about the inheritance tax?*

A: The inheritance tax should be eliminated. It is not
necessary under a system with comprehensive, wa-
tertight taxation of income, which taxes all income
once. An inheritance tax constitutes double taxation, which violates a sacred principle of sound tax
policy.

Q: *Wouldn't it be a good idea to broaden the tax base
by including gifts, life insurance proceeds, inheritances, and so forth?*

A: No. The tax base for the flat tax is carefully chosen
to provide the most efficient economic incentives.
Further broadening to the listed items would be
double taxation. Gifts represent a transfer of income
that has already been taxed, and there is no reason
to tax it again. Life insurance proceeds are a mixture
of interest earnings, which have already been taxed
by the business tax, and return of premiums, which
were paid from income already taxed. Inheritances
are just a special form of gifts.

ECONOMIC AND SOCIAL BENEFITS

Q: *How will the flat tax change the spending and savings patterns of individuals and businesses?*

A: The improved, uniform investment and savings incentives provided by universal first-year write-offs will channel capital into its most productive uses because all returns to investment will be taxed at the same low 19 percent rate. No tax shelters can provide a higher return or lower tax rates than regular business investments subject to the simple flat tax. Applying the same tax rate to all taxpayers will prevent the widespread abuse of tax shelters that divert savings from their efficient destinations. Dramatic reductions in marginal tax rates will stimulate investment and work effort and draw activities out of the underground economy and into the more efficient market economy.

The flat tax will dramatically reduce the disincentive costs faced by individuals and businesses. These costs run in the tens of billions of dollars. When the disincentives of high rates are eliminated, real incomes, wages, and living standards will rise.

Q: *How much will we save by each year having to fill out only the two postcard returns in place of Form 1040 and all its schedules?*

A: A conservative estimate, based on careful studies commissioned by the IRS, is $50 billion. Some estimates are even higher. This is a staggering amount of money, equal to 10 percent of all individual income taxes. The simple flat tax eliminates most of this cost.

Q: *It sounds like the flat tax is just a clever ploy to raise taxes on the already overburdened American tax-*

payer. Aren't we actually better off with the present system, with all its defects?

A: Actually, the present system won't stand still long enough for taxpayers to understand and cope with all of its details. Remember, the top rate was 28 percent in 1986. It rose to 31 percent in 1991 and to 39.6 percent in 1993. Other details of the tax code also change just about every year.

Almost everyone is better off under the flat tax. The poorest families are completely exempt from the income tax, which is much better than their treatment under current law. Some middle-income and rich taxpayers will pay more because they have been aggressive users of shelters and itemized deductions, but any losses they face will be offset in future years by dramatically improved incentives.

Remember, the current tax system imposes compliance costs of $50 billion or more and disincentive costs of $50 billion or more, and it engenders hostility among Americans toward their government. The economy as a whole will be better off by well over $100 billion, perhaps as much as $200 billion or more, if we move to the flat tax. This sum is almost equal to the annual federal budget deficit, about which so much has been made.

Q: *How will the flat tax help the American economy grow?*

A: Every study we can find shows that lower tax rates on businesses and employees, by improving incentives, increase the supply of labor, capital, and entrepreneurship. More people will join the labor force or work longer hours, especially in two-earner households; more people will risk their capital; and more people will undertake risky ventures to start up new businesses. Today's double tax on business income means that entrepreneurs face rates as high as 60 percent on the rewards for successful innovation. A low flat tax of 19 percent will attract bright people to innovation and away from tax-sheltered activities favored by the current system. The flat tax provides dramatically improved incentives for capital formation, through its first-year write-off provision, an important source of growth in the longer run.

The evidence compiled by the country's leading tax experts is that the flat tax will increase real incomes about 6 percent in the seven years after it is adopted. Higher growth will generate more revenues than the current system, which means that future deficits will be lower. To the extent that lower deficits imply lower interest rates, due to diminished federal borrowing, the economy will benefit.

Q: *What will happen to the stock market when the flat-tax law goes into effect?*

A: We expect the stock market to rise. Lower tax rates on corporations, coupled with the elimination of both the taxation of dividends and/or capital gains, will increase corporate income and make ownership of stock more attractive. High-growth firms that can make productive use of the 100 percent first-year write-off will attract investor interest and command higher price-to-earnings ratios than slower-growth firms. In contrast, companies that depend heavily on interest deductions and depreciation on existing plant and equipment may look less attractive to investors, but these firms can be protected under transition arrangements that permit such firms to utilize those benefits that will be eliminated under the flat tax.

Q: *What about the international value of the dollar?*

A: Adopting the flat tax would lower interest rates in the United States to the level of tax-free bonds. To an extent that would depend on the monetary policies of other major nations, world interest rates would fall in tandem. (Financial markets are global, and changes in U.S. interest rates immediately affect bonds and stocks in all major world markets.) If world rates do not fall as much as U.S. rates, the dollar would depreciate relative to other currencies. Offsetting this effect is the inflow of foreign investment, seeking to take advantage of the improved investment climate in the United States, which would bid up the value of the dollar. In the longer run, interest rates around the world will tend to equalize, and the effects of the tax reform on exchange rates will disappear.

RETIREMENT

Q: *How are existing IRA and Keogh retirement accounts treated under the flat tax?*

A: IRA and Keogh accounts have provided benefits to a limited fraction of taxpayers of the same type that the flat tax would provide to all taxpayers. Under the flat tax, they would be treated exactly as under the current system, except that the tax rate would usually be much lower. When the accounts begin to pay retirement benefits, those benefits would be taxed as compensation. It would no longer be necessary to impose a minimum age for the payment of benefits. Holders of IRA and Keogh accounts could elect to draw benefits at any time and pay the tax due. For the future, IRA and Keogh accounts would not be necessary because the taxation of interest at the business rather than the personal level would give any form of savings the same advantage that IRAs and Keoghs have today, namely, tax-deferred compounding.

Q: *What about Social Security? How does it fit in with the flat tax?*

A: First of all, it is worth pointing out that the Social Security tax is a completely successful flat tax. Since its inception in the 1930s, it has remained remarkably free from complicating amendments. Indeed, its history shows that we are capable of keeping a tax flat.

Under the flat tax, the employer's contribution

would be treated like other fringe benefits—it would not be deductible from the business tax. As at present, the employee's contribution would be included in taxable income under the wage tax. Thus all Social Security contributions would be included in the tax base. However, Social Security benefits would be completely untaxed. We would eliminate the current partial taxation of benefits for higher-income taxpayers. Eliminating the employer's deduction for contributions is a better way to tax benefits.

Q: *Interest on the savings in my life insurance policy is excluded from current taxation under today's law. What will happen to the life insurance industry and the value of my insurance when taxation of all interest is eliminated?*

A: As far as you are concerned, the tax benefits you are enjoying will continue—there will be no taxes on the interest you are earning. Furthermore, when your insurance pays off, you will not have to pay income tax on the interest component, as you do under current law. As far as the industry is concerned, taxing its interest earnings and deducting its interest payments will end. Only its actual insurance premiums will count as income, not the saving that goes with some types of insurance, and only its payoff for death and other insured events will count as business expenses.

POLITICS AND THE FLAT TAX

Q: *Does the flat tax have any chance of being adopted?*

A: We remain optimistic, despite vigorous opposition from those individuals and special interests who have an ideological or financial stake in the current tax system. The flat tax has received support from a broad cross section of past and present politicians, along with endorsements from many prominent editorial writers. The list of those who expressed interest in the flat tax in 1982 includes some surprising entries: Lloyd Bentsen, former chairman of the Senate Finance Committee and President Clinton's first secretary of the treasury; Leon Panetta, former member of the House of Representatives and President Clinton's first head of the Office of Management and Budget; former and current Congressmen Philip Crane, Ron Paul, John Duncan, and George Hansen; and former and current Senators Charles Grassley, Jesse Helms, Dennis DeConcini, Steve Symms, and Dan Quayle.

In 1992, the most noteworthy proponent was former California governor Jerry Brown, who made the flat tax the economic centerpiece of his run for the presidency in 1992. When both the New York Times and the Wall Street Journal endorse the Hall-Rabushka flat tax on successive days, you can be sure the idea commands great interest and support.

In 1994, Congressman Dick Armey of Texas introduced HR 4585, which included a 17 percent flat tax modeled after Hall-Rabushka. We expect that many members of Congress will give the flat tax serious consideration during 1995–1996.

Q: *So why isn't the flat tax the law of the land?*

A: Remember, there are thousands of lobbyists in Washington, D.C., who work full time to preserve tax benefits for their interest groups and clients. They contribute large sums to the campaign coffers of the two congressional tax-writing committees. They fiercely resist the flat tax because it would put them all out of business.

We are prepared to support, on this one occasion, a federally subsidized retraining program for those several hundred thousand bright people, despite our general opposition to government intervention in the economy. Most of them won't need it, but it is a small price to pay for a low, simple flat tax. We suspect that the overwhelming majority of Americans agree.

Remember, too, that the reduction in the top marginal rate from 70 percent in 1980 to 28 percent in 1986 took much of the steam out of the flat-tax movement. However, now that the top rate has been raised to 39.6 percent, there is growing support for lowering high marginal rates.

Q: *What is your strategy for getting the flat tax adopted?*

A: We believe that the main political support for the flat tax will come from millions of taxpayers who will insist that dozens of forms and hundreds of pages of tax instructions and regulations be replaced with two simple postcards. The flat tax will ultimately succeed because of the American taxpayer's demand for a true simplicity. We also believe that the politics of envy will not withstand a convincing demonstration that the flat tax is fair.

Notes and References

The *Declaration of Independence* is on display in the main lobby of the National Archives in Washington, D.C.

Standard sources of tax forms, laws, and regulations include *Marten's Law of Federal Income Taxation*, which consists of eighteen loose-leaf volumes of tax forms and laws and eight volumes of accompanying regulations; Commerce Clearing House, Inc., some sixteen volumes of forms and laws and six volumes of regulations; and West Publishing Company's annual or biannual reports on "Acts Amendatory of the Internal Revenue Code" published as *Internal Revenue Acts: Text and Legislative History.*

The following journals can be found in the Law Library of Stanford University and in the offices of many tax practitioners: *American Federal Tax Reports, Journal of Corporate Taxation, Journal of Taxation, Major Tax Planning, Monthly Digest of Tax Articles, National Tax Association Proceedings, National Tax Journal, New York University Institute on Federal Taxation, Practical Tax Lawyer, Prentice Hall Federal Tax Handbook, The Review of Taxation of Individuals, Tax Adviser, Taxation, Taxation for Lawyers, Tax Court Digest, Tax Court Memorandum Decisions, Taxes, Tax Facts, Tax Guide, Tax Law Review, Tax Lawyer, Tax Notes, Tax Planning*

Tips, U.S. Tax Cases, U.S. Tax Court Reports, and *U.S. Tax Week*.

A comprehensive review of all the studies that attempt to measure the costs associated with the federal income tax appears in James L. Payne, *Costly Returns: The Burdens of the U.S. Tax System* (San Francisco: Institute for Contemporary Studies Press, 1993). Payne summarizes the estimates of compliance costs that appear in the following studies: Joel Slemrod and Nikki Sorum, "The Compliance Cost of the U.S. Individual Income Tax System," *National Tax Journal* 37 (December 1984): 462–65; Arthur D. Little, Inc., *Development of Methodology for Estimating the Taxpayer Paperwork Burden* (Washington, D.C.: Internal Revenue Service, 1988), pp. III–23; James T. Iocozzia and Garrick R. Shear, "Trends in Taxpayer Paperwork Burden," in Internal Revenue Service, *Trend Analyses and Related Statistics, 1989 Update* (Washington, D.C.: U.S. Government Printing Office, 1989), p. 56; *Annual Reports* of the commissioner of the Internal Revenue Service; and a variety of other IRS memoranda.

The following studies attempt to estimate the disincentive costs of the U.S. federal income tax: Edgar K. Browning, "On the Marginal Welfare Cost of Taxation," *American Economic Review* 77 (March 1987): 21; Jerry A. Hausman, "Labor Supply," in Henry J. Aaron and Joseph A. Pechman, eds., *How Taxes Affect Economic Behavior* (Washington, D.C.: Brookings Institution, 1981), p. 61; Charles Stuart, "Welfare Costs per Dollar of Additional Tax Revenue in the United States," *American Economic Review* 74 (June 1984): 358; Roger H.

Gordon and Burton G. Malkiel, "Corporation Finance," in Aaron and Pechman, eds., *How Taxes Affect Economic Behavior*, p. 178; Jane G. Gravelle and Laurence J. Kotlikoff, "The Incidence and Efficiency Costs of Corporate Taxation When Corporate and Noncorporate Firms Produce the Same Good," *Journal of Political Economy* 97 (August 1989): 774, table 6; Charles L. Ballard, John B. Shoven, and John Whalley, "General Equilibrium Computations of the Marginal Welfare Costs of Taxes in the United States," *American Economic Review*, March 1985, p. 135, table 3; Dale W. Jorgenson and Kun-Young Yun, "The Excess Burden of Taxation in the U.S." (paper prepared for presentation at the Coopers & Lybrand Foundation symposium U.S. Tax Policy for the 1990s, New York, November 7–8, 1990), p. 18; Michael J. Boskin, "Efficiency Aspects of the Differential Tax Treatment of Market and Household Economic Activity," *Journal of Public Economics* 4 (1975): 12; Martin Feldstein and Joel Slemrod, "Inflation and the Excess Taxation of Capital Gains on Corporate Stock," *National Tax Journal* 31 (1978): 107–18; Michael J. Boskin, "Taxation, Saving, and the Rate of Interest," *Journal of Political Economy* 86 (1978):S3–S27; Martin Feldstein, "Tax Rules and Business Investment," in Martin Feldstein, ed., *Taxes and Capital Formation* (Chicago: University of Chicago Press, 1987), pp. 63–72; and Roger H. Gordon and Joel Slemrod, "Do We Collect Any Revenue from Taxing Capital Income?" in Lawrence H. Summers, ed., *Tax Policy and the Economy* 2 (Cambridge, Mass.: MIT Press, 1988), p. 120.

Official and unofficial estimates exist on the extent of tax evasion. Official estimates include *Estimates of Income Unreported on Individual Tax Returns*, Department of the Treasury, Internal Revenue Service, Publication 1104 (9-79); *Internal Revenue Service's 1988 Report on the "Tax Gap"* (hearing before the Subcommittee on Oversight of the Committee on Ways and Means, U.S. House of Representatives, 100th Congress, 2d Session, March 17, 1988); and General Accounting Office, *Who's Not Filing Income Tax Returns? IRS Needs Better Ways to Find Them and Collect Their Taxes* (Washington, D.C., July 11, 1979). Academic and popular accounts are contained in Vito Tanzi, ed., *The Underground Economy in the United States and Abroad* (Lexington, Mass.: D.C. Heath, 1982); Dan Bawly, *The Subterranean Economy* (New York: McGraw-Hill, 1982); and Carl P. Simon and Ann D. Witte, *Beating the System: The Underground Economy* (Boston: Auburn House, 1982).

To determine the extent of tax avoidance, we recommend careful examination of the annual Internal Revenue Service publication titled *Statistics of Income, Individual Income Tax Returns* (Washington, D.C.). It lists the value of every deduction taxpayers declare on their returns by category. It provides evidence on the overall size of tax shelters in published information on itemized deductions, partnership returns, and other business tax returns. The quarterly *Statistics of Income Bulletin*, published by the IRS, contains detailed analyses of tax returns. The total aggregate value of all tax subsidy items in the economy is enumeraged by category in each year's federal budget in *Special Analysis G. Tax Expenditures: The Budget of the United States Government*, Office of Management and Budget, Executive Office of the President, annual report.

The history of U.S. income taxes appears in Joseph A. Pechman, *Federal Tax Policy*, 4th ed. (Washington, D.C.: Brookings Institution, 1983), pp. 290–92; Bill Bradley, *The Fair Tax* (New York: Pocket Books, 1984), pp. 68–89; and John F. Witte, *The Politics and Development of the Federal Income Tax* (Madison: University of Wisconsin Press, 1985). Details of recent tax increases are found in the various conference reports of the U.S. Congress published by the U.S. Government Printing Office.

2. WHAT'S FAIR ABOUT TAXES?

Two general all-purpose references for calculating the size and growth of government taxes and spending are the *Economic Report of the President*, published each January, and the quarterly *Treasury Bulletin*, published by the Treasury Department.

A history of tax rates in all the world's main civilizations is found in Charles Adams, *For Good and Evil: The Impact of Taxes on the Course of Civilization* (London, New York, Lanham, Md.: Madison Books, 1993).

Statistics on the distribution of the tax burden by income categories are published annually by the Tax Foundation. The IRS publication *Statistics of Income, Individual Income Tax Returns*, analyzes the distribution of taxes by adjusted gross income categories for all sources of income and most major deductions.

The distributional effects of Secretary of the Treasury Andrew Mellon's 1920s tax cuts are analyzed in James Gwartney and Richard Stroup, "Tax Cuts: Who Shoulders the Burden," *Economic Review*, March 1982, pp. 19–27. The distributional effects of President John F. Kennedy's tax cuts in the early 1960s are analyzed in Lawrence B. Lindsey, *The Growth Experiment: How the New Tax Policy Is Transforming the U.S. Economy* (New York: Basic Books, 1990), pp. 28–40. The distributional effects of President Ronald Reagan's marginal tax rate cuts in the 1980s are analyzed by the Statistics of Income Division, Internal Revenue Service, Washington, D.C.

3. THE POSTCARD TAX RETURN

Sources for table 3.1 are: line 1: *Economic Report of the President*, table B-1; line 2: Table B-23; line 3: Gross domestic product arising from households and institutions, table B-10; line 4: Table B-25; line 5: Nonresidential fixed investment plus portion of residential investment for nonowner occupied, table B-1; line 8: Family allowances are calculated as the difference between the revenue that would be generated by a 19 percent rate applied to the business tax base, line 6 plus wages, salaries, and pensions, line 4, and the actual tax revenue, line 14, all divided by .19. This guarantees that the revenue from the flat tax is exactly the same as actual revenue.; line 12: Table B-78; line 13: Table B-78.

Calculation of the number and value of the personal allowances proceeded in the following way: Based on data in *Statistics of Income Basic Tables*, 1991, table 2.4, we inferred the number of allowances as follows:

Type of Allowance	Number in 1991 (millions)	Number in 1995 (millions)	Relative Amount
Single	52	54	1.00
Married	49	51	1.75
Head of household	14	14	1.50
Dependent	78	81	0.50

The relative amount is our judgment about the relative dollar values of the allowances. By weighting each type of allowance by its relative weight, we calculate that there will be 204 million allowance units in 1995. Dividing this number into the total value of allowances from line 8 of table 1, we calculate that each allowance unit is $9,377. The calculations of the allowances for Form 1 are as follows:

Type of Allowance	Relative Amount	Extra Calculated Value	Rounded Value
Single	1.00	9,377	9,500
Married	1.75	16,410	16,500
Head of household	1.50	14,066	14,000
Dependent	0.50	4,689	4,500

Operating data for General Motors, Intel, and the First National Bank of Rocky Mount came from their annual reports for 1993.

Total depreciation deductions under the personal

and corporate income taxes in 1992 appear in *Statistics of Income Bulletin*, summer 1994, pp. 124–28.

The calculation of alternative allowances permitted by alternative tax rates is based on the logic set forth above for the calculation of the revenue-neutral total amount of allowances corresponding to a given tax rate:

Allowances = business tax base + wages, salaries, and pensions − (required revenue/flat-tax rate)

The alternative combinations of investment write-offs and tax rates that would all raise the same revenue are calculated by modifying the tax base so that only a portion of investment is subtracted. The modified base is divided by the required revenue to obtain the necessary tax rate.

4. THE FLAT TAX AND THE ECONOMY

Data on labor force participation are from table A-13, Employment Status of the Civilian Noninstitutional Population by Age, Sex, and Race, *Employment and Earnings*, winter 1993/94.

On taxes and labor supply, see the *Journal of Human Resources*, Special Issue on Taxation and Labor Supply 25, no. 3 (summer 1990), and Jerry Hausman, "Taxes and Labor Supply," in Alan J. Auerbach and Martin Feldstein, eds., *Handbook of Public Economics*, vol. 1, chap. 4 (Amsterdam: North Holland, 1985), pp. 213–63.

On the effect of a flat-rate tax on capital formation, see Alan J. Auerbach, Laurence J. Kotlikoff, and Jonathan Skinner, "The Efficiency Gains from Dynamic Tax Reform," *International Economic Review* 24, no. 1 (February 1983): 81–100, and Auerbach and Kotlikoff, *Dynamic Fiscal Policy* (Cambridge: Cambridge University Press), 1987.

Data on taxes and exemptions by income category come from *Statistics of Income*, table 1.2.

Data on nonwage income reported on personal income tax forms come from *Statistics of Income*, Individual Returns 1991, table 1.4, All Returns: Sources of Income, Adjustments, and Tax Items, by Size of Adjusted Gross Income.

Data on charitable contributions are from the American Association of Fund-Raising Counsel, Inc., *Giving USA*, 1994. Data on deductions of charitable contributions come from *Statistics of Income*, various issues.

Appendix:
A Flat-Tax Law

A BILL TO AMEND the Internal Revenue Code to implement a flat-rate tax system.

Be it enacted by the Senate and House of Representatives of the United States of America in Congress assembled

That (a) subtitle A of the Internal Revenue Code is amended to read as follows.

SECTION 1.   SHORT TITLE

This act may be cited as the "Tax Reform Act of 1995."

Subtitle A—Income Taxes

CHAPTER 1. COMPUTATION OF TAXABLE INCOME

Sec. 101. Compensation defined

(a) In general. Compensation means all cash amounts paid by an employer or received by an employee, including wages, pensions, bonuses, prizes, and awards.

(b) Certain items included. Compensation includes

  (1) The cash equivalent of any financial instrument conveyed to an employee, measured as market value at the time of conveyance

  (2) Workman's compensation and other payments for injuries or other compensation for damages

(c) Certain items excluded. Compensation excludes

  (1) Reimbursements to employees by employers for business expenses paid by the taxpayer in connection with performance by him or her of services as an employee

  (2) Goods and services provided to employees by employers, including but not limited to medical benefits, insurance, meals, housing, recreational facilities, and other fringe benefits

  (3) Wages, salaries, and other payments for services performed outside the United States

Sec. 102. Business receipts defined

Business receipts are the receipts of a business from the sale or exchange of products or services produced in or passing through the United States. Business receipts include

  (1) Gross revenue, excluding sales and excise taxes, from the sale of goods and services

  (2) Fees, commissions, and similar receipts, if not reported as compensation

  (3) Gross rents

  (4) Royalties

  (5) Gross receipts from the sale of plant, equipment, and land

  (6) The market value of goods, services, plant, equipment, or land provided to its owners or employees

  (7) The market value of goods, services, and equipment delivered from the United States to points outside the United States, if not included in sales

  (8) The market value of goods and services provided to depositors, insurance policyholders, and others with a financial claim upon the business, if not included in sales

Sec. 103. Cost of business inputs defined

(a) In general. The cost of business inputs is the actual cost of purchases of goods, services, and materials required for business purposes.

(b) Certain items included. The cost of business inputs includes

  (1) The actual amount paid for goods, services, and materials, whether or not resold during the year

  (2) The market value of business inputs brought into the United States

  (3) The actual cost, if reasonable, of travel and entertainment expenses for business purposes

(c) Certain items excluded. The cost of business inputs

excludes purchases of goods and services provided to employees or owners, unless these are included in business receipts.

Sec. 104. Cost of capital equipment, structures, and land defined

The cost of capital equipment, structures, and land includes any purchases of these items for business purposes. In the case of equipment brought into the United States, the cost is the market value at the time of entry into the United States.

Sec. 105. Business taxable income defined

Business taxable income is business receipts less the cost of business inputs, less compensation paid to employees, and less the cost of capital equipment, structures, and land.

CHAPTER 2. DETERMINATION OF TAX LIABILITY

Sec. 201. Personal allowances.
Sec. 202. Compensation tax.
Sec. 203. Business tax.

Sec. 201. Personal allowances

(a) In general. For the year 1995, personal allowances are

(1) For married taxpayers filing jointly, $16,500. A taxpayer is considered married if he was married at the end of the year or his/her spouse died during the year.

    (2) For heads of households, $14,000. A taxpayer is head of a household if he is not married and maintains as his home a household that is the principal home of a dependent son, stepson, daughter, stepdaughter, mother, or father of the taxpayer and the taxpayer provides more than half the support for the dependent.

    (3) For single taxpayers, $9,500.

    (4) For each dependent, $4,500. A dependent is a son, stepson, daughter, stepdaughter, mother, or father of the taxpayer for whom the taxpayer provides more than half support.

(b) Adjustments. Each year, personal allowances rise by the proportional increase from the beginning to the end of the immediately preceding year in the Consumer Price Index.

Sec. 202. Compensation tax

Each individual employed at any time during the year will pay a tax of 19 percent of his compensation, less his personal allowance, or no tax if his compensation is less than his personal allowance.

Sec. 203. Business tax

(a) Business defined. Each sole proprietorship, partnership, and corporation constitutes a business. Any organization or individual not specifically exempt under chapter 3, with business receipts, is a business.

(b) Computation of tax. Each business will pay a tax of 19 percent of its business taxable income or zero if business taxable income is negative.

(c) Filing units. A business may file any number of business tax returns for its various subsidiaries or other units, provided that all business receipts are reported in the aggregate and provided that each expenditure for business inputs is reported on no more than one return.

(d) Carry forward of losses. When business taxable income is negative, the negative amounts may be used to offset positive taxes in future years. The amount carried forward from one year to the next is augmented according to an interest rate equal to the average daily yield on three-month Treasury Bills during the first year. There is no limit to the amount or the duration of the carry forward.

CHAPTER 3. EXEMPT ORGANIZATIONS

Sec. 301. Exempt organizations

Organizations exempt from the business tax are

(1) State and local governments, and their subsidiary units

(2) Educational, religious, charitable, philanthropic, cultural, and community service organizations that do not return income to individual and corporate owners

CHAPTER 4. WITHHOLDING

Sec. 401. Withholding

Each employer, including exempt organizations, will withhold from the wages, salaries, and pensions of its employees and remit to the Internal Revenue Service an amount computed as follows: 19 percent of the excess of compensation in each pay period over the employee's annual personal allowance, prorated for the length of the pay period. Every employee will receive a credit against tax for the amount withheld.

(b) The amendment made by this section shall apply to taxable years beginning after December 31, 1994.

About the Authors

ROBERT E. HALL holds a joint position endowed by Robert and Carole McNeil as a senior fellow at the Hoover Institution and a professor in the economics department, Stanford University. He is a member of the National Academy of Sciences and a fellow of the American Academy of Arts and Sciences, the Econometric Society and the Society of Labor Economists. When not promoting tax reform, Hall spends his time puzzling over the behavior of the U.S. economy, with a career-long concern about the ups and downs of employment and unemployment and a more recent interest in the volatility of the stock market. He is currently working on how the public will pay for the rapid rise in spending on health care late in life. He lives in Menlo Park with his economist wife and two cats.

ALVIN RABUSHKA, the David and Joan Traitel Senior Fellow at the Hoover Institution, works in the public policy areas of taxation in the United States and abroad, economic development in the Pacific Rim countries, and the economies of Central and Eastern Europe. He does missionary work in Central and Eastern Europe, promoting the flat tax. In recent years, he has turned his attention to colonial America. His forthcoming book, *Taxation in Colonial America, 1607–1775*, is scheduled for publication by Princeton University Press in February 2008. He lives on the Stanford campus with his landscape enthusiast wife.

Index